JOEL M. LERNER'S

101

Home Landscaping

IDEAS*

*FOR EVERY SHAPE & SIZE LOT!

HPBooks

PRICE STERN SLOAN

Los Angeles

HPBooks
A division of Price Stern Sloan, Inc.
360 North La Cienega Boulevard
Los Angeles, California 90048

9 8 7 6 5 4 3 2

Library of Congress Cataloging-in-Publication Data

Lerner, Joel M., 1947—
   Joel M. Lerner's 101 home landscaping ideas.

   1. Landscape gardening.   2. Landscape architecture.
I. Title.   II. Title: One hundred one home landscaping ideas.
III. Title: One hundred and one home landscaping ideas.
IV. Title: Home landscaping ideas.
SB473.L45   1988   712'.6   87-21258
ISBN 0-89586-721-4 (pbk.)

LERNSCAPE® is a registered trademark of Joel M. Lerner Environmental Design. Concept by Richard C. Levy. Designed and illustrated by Jan Tadlock Papandrea.

CONTENTS

Dedicated to Sandy and Jason.

Author's Biography

Joel M. Lerner is a nationally recognized designer, author, and lecturer. In addition, he is the father of LERNSCAPING®, a unique process of environmental design which matches people's personalities to their properties.

President of Environmental Design, with offices in Chevy Chase, Maryland; Harrisburg, Pennsylvania and Sarasota, Florida; Joel's clientele range from high rise apartments and public hospitals to residential estates and townhouse properties. His firm specializes in landscape consulting and design.

Nicknamed the "Garden Guru," Joel's designs have been taught at the university level and are used by professional design companies nationwide. He has lectured at The U.S. National Arboretum, George Washington University, University of Maryland and The Smithsonian Institution. Joel hosted the radio show "Landscaping with Lerner," and was named "Designer of the Month" in the February, 1988 issue of *Home Mechanix* magazine.

He is also the author of the critically acclaimed books, *101 Townhouse Garden Designs* (HPBooks, 1985) and *101 Designs With Houseplants* (SANJO Press, 1987). His articles and designs have appeared in *Garden Design, Architectural Designs, Gardens, Early American Life* magazines, and *The Washington Post* as well as many other newspapers.

Environmental Design sponsors the annual popular conference in Washington, D.C. entitled Leaving No Stone Unturned, at which landscape professionals intergrate ideas and exchange philosophies and theories.

"Great guide to get people stimulated to maximize the use of their space and make it fit their lifestyle. It makes their property work for them, rather than making them work for their property."

David T. Scheid
Executive Director
United States Botanic Garden
Washington, D.C.

"An exciting book that proves that a little imagination can transform the commonplace into the extraordinary."

Stephen Wagner
Editor
Architectural Designs
New York, N.Y.

LERN•SCAPE (lern' skāp) vt: to put you in touch with your property and make it reflect the essence of your personality.

INTRODUCTION

LANDSCAPING is the greatest visual impact one can make on a property.

LERNSCAPING® is a unique do-it-yourself environmental design program that matches one's personality to a property.

And when landscaping and LERNSCAPING are combined, the result is the most engaging, practical and personalized property imaginable.

101 Home Landscaping Ideas (*For Every Shape & Size Lot*) will acquaint you with the basics of landscape design and show you how to develop E.S.P.—Extra Special Property!

There is an infinite number of design concepts to fit a property, but the best ideas are those that fit your lifestyle requirements. And you are the best qualified person to decide what activities will take place in your garden and what "look" you want.

Part I of this book offers myriad basic design considerations and self-help checklists to put you on the road to discovery.

Part II consists of 101 plan-view designs, all drawn to the same scale (1″ = 20′). Use them as they are or mix and match to create literally thousands of varied designs.

Part III features hundreds of plants commonly sold in many parts of the country. It is by no means a definitive list and should be used only as a core for possibilities.

Once you have a picture of what you want for your property, I encourage you to consult a professional at a local garden center, and review your ideas.

My plans are not meant to be end-product, plug-in gardens. They are meant to provide goals and ideas, and serve as sensible examples for designing beautiful properties.

Joel M. Lerner

5 EASY STEPS TO LERNSCAPING®

PHILOSOPHY OF LERNSCAPE DESIGN

The basic philosophy of LERNSCAPE® design is to work with the environment, to create functional use and beauty. In this way maximum benefits can be derived from the land.

Using the following LERNSCAPE® guidelines and checklists, you can make the same decisions as professional designers, and thereby make the most of your property.

IDEA DEVELOPMENT

Thumbing through this book will offer a few hundred ideas to start, but get around and see what others in your area have done as well.

Begin by developing some perception of what you want. Landscape design ideas are everywhere. Arboreta, public gardens and garden centers aren't the only excellent resources. Others are shopping malls, office buildings, industrial parks, apartments, hospitals, schools and neighborhoods. As you start to notice the landscape while going about your daily routine, you will begin to develop design ideas.

As your ideas develop, think in general terms about the look you wish to achieve: for example, walls, hedges, patios, walks, flowering borders, vegetables, and so on. There's plenty of time to get specific plant suggestions once you know what you generally want.

PERSONAL CONSIDERATIONS

Use the checklists that follow to put your personality into the design. Include every whim and fancy. I have tried to include everything you may want. Use the checklist to stimulate original ideas of your own.

CONSIDERATIONS FOR COMFORT

After reading through the checklists and deciding your personal desires, try incorporating some of the following concepts, which are known to promote comfort in the garden.

Create Maximum Use—The more features you can include into the design, the more usable the space becomes, but be sure to integrate these features with one another. Flowers, vegetables, herbs, pools, hot tubs and patios will all fit together if you stick with one or two basic themes and use similar construction materials.

Create Spatial Enclosure—It's human nature to be more comfortable in privacy. If you entertain, enjoy sunning or have unpleasant views, you may wish to devise strong enclosures such as hedges and fences. If there is a pleasant view or you wish to integrate your landscaping into the surroundings, then use weaker enclosures, such as shade trees and smaller groupings of plants.

Garden or Landscape to the Horizon—All the landscaping within your view should be noticed and considered for design. Whatever your view, make the best of it, or invent ways to overcome it. Generally, pleasant views can be framed to be enjoyed and unpleasant ones screened.

Make Your Garden Inviting—A smooth indoor/outdoor design relationship will integrate the house with the environment. A patio or deck near a spacious entry will offer the incentive and make it more comfortable for you to go into the garden.

Design Problems—This could be harsh drying winter winds, hot drying sun, poor drainage, noise or simply plants that are susceptible to disease or marginally hardy. Any design problems that you can overcome or modify will make your garden more comfortable.

CONSIDERATIONS FOR INTEREST

There are many ways to create visual interest in the garden with unique plant "personalities." Think about how a plant changes from season to season. Consider flower, fruit, foliage, as well as branches and bark, for winter interest. Include plants in your design that have more than one season's interest. Go to garden centers, gardens and arboreta and see how plants look at different times of the year. There are many excellent reference books at your local bookstore or library that also depict flowering cycles.

Distinctive Qualities—Choose plants for their distinctive qualities. Look at form. Is it fan shaped, vase shaped, or does it grow with a rounded or pyramidal habit? Plants can display many forms.

Size—Size of plants is another important factor. Mature size of the plantings determines whether they will fit a given space. This is a point that we often forget when the plant is purchased knee high, but we discover it as the walks lift, roofs rot, entries block and drains clog from overgrown, mature plants.

Texture—Texture and color also have a role in the plant's personality. Leaf size usually determines the texture. Small-leaved or needled plants tend to project a fine textured look, while larger-leaved plants appear coarser. The design is usually more harmonious when similarly textured plants are used together. Fine textures tend to recede from the viewer, giving a more spacious appearance. Coarse textures advance toward the viewer, creating a more enclosed feeling.

Color—Color gives the extra touch that makes gardens noticeable. Use favorite colors, or use cool colors (green, blue, violet) to recede from the viewer, and warm colors (red, orange, yellow) to advance toward the viewer. Coordinate blooming times throughout the growing season, but massed plantings of the same variety should all be the same color, and bloom at the same time.

Planes—Another consideration that contributes to the garden's artistry is the use of all levels of design space. Design for the ground, vertical and overhead planes. Gardens with this overall balance are far more interesting.

Senses—Appeal to all your senses. Appearance, fragrance, taste, touch and sound must all be considered. Fragrant plants and flowers; fruits, vegetables and herbs; furry and smooth-leaved plants; rustling leaves and the flow of water—don't leave anything out. Even the interplay of reflected light is a consideration. After all, there's no need to be practical on paper. You're only limited by your imagination.

Put my LERNSCAPING® design principles and concepts into practice. Thumb through the 101 designs. Develop *your* ideas. Make *your* personal considerations. Turn your garden into an interesting, comfortable, practical and satisfying extension of *your* personality.

Part I
CHECKLISTS

PART I

The designer checklist is easy to follow and written to help organize your ideas. Read through it and fill in the areas that apply to you. Note the section entitled, "Property Characteristics." These are points to consider throughout the entire job. For example, poor surface drainage or damaged underground utilities can create unneeded complications and costs. Landscape professionals are readily available should questions occur during your planning process.

CHECKLIST A:
DESIGN CONSIDERATIONS

Budget _____

Design Style (Optional)
____ Oriental
____ English
____ American Colonial
____ Modern
____ Other

Design Motif
____ Formal
____ Informal
____ Rectilinear
____ Curvilinear
____ Contemporary
____ Rustic
____ Other

Design Functions
Entertainment   ( ) Yes   ( ) No
_____ Frequency
_____ Number

Seating   ( ) Yes   ( ) No
_____ Permanent
_____ Temporary
Patio   ( ) Yes   ( ) No
_____ Size
_____ Construction Material
Accessories   ( ) Yes   ( ) No
_____ Water
_____ Lighting
_____ Statuary

Other Structures   ( ) Yes   ( ) No
____ Trellis   ____ Fences
____ Pergola/Arbor   ____ Steps
____ Barbecue   ____ Walks
____ Pool, Hot Tub, Whirlpool ____ Other
____ Conservatory

Children   ( ) Yes   ( ) No
____ Number   ____ Playground/
____ Ages   Entertainment

Interests
Athletic Activities _____

Nature Activities _____

Cultural Activities _____

Other Activities _____

Utility

____ Pets
____ Clothesline
____ Firewood
____ Service Area
____ Storage Area
____ Tool Shed
____ Potting Shed
____ Greenhouse
____ Compost
____ Parking
____ Garage
____ Other

Construction Material

____ Wood
____ Brick
____ Concrete
____ Slate
____ Rock
____ Metal
____ Fiberglass
____ Ceramic
____ Reed or Fabric
____ Other

Type of Plant Material

____ Foliage Plants
____ Flowering Plants
____ Fragrant Plants
____ Perennial Flowers
____ Annual Flowers
____ Bulbs
____ Cut Flowers
____ Vegetables
____ Herbs
____ Fruits
____ Other

Use of Plant Material

____ Privacy
____ Noise Reduction
____ Pollution Reduction
____ Energy Efficiency
____ Attract Wildlife
____ Discourage Wildlife
____ Aesthetics

Plant Preferences

Favorite _____

Unfavorite _____

_____ Evergreen

_____ Deciduous

Color Preferences _____

Season Preferences _____

Primary Times Garden Will Be Used _____

Maintenance

Do you plan to maintain the property yourself? _____

How much time can you devote? _____

_____

What do you enjoy doing in the garden? _____

_____

What don't you enjoy doing in the garden? _____

_____

Property Characteristics

Measurements of Design Area _____

Compass Points and Hours of Sun _____

Surface Drainage _____

Location of Underground Utilities _____

Pleasant Views _____

Features Worth Retaining _____

Unpleasant Views _____

Other Characteristics _____

CHECKLIST NOTES:

_____

_____

_____

_____

_____

_____

_____

_____

_____

_____

The garden activity and style list is designed to help you decide what mood your garden will convey and what activities will take place there. Go through and check the categories that most closely match your interests. Check any number of categories that you wish. The following list helps locate the designs.

CHECKLIST B:
GARDEN ACTIVITY and STYLE

Category

Kindergardens _____	16-20
Pets _____	21-23
Low Maintanence _____	24-31
Storage and Aesthetics _____	32-38
Privacy and Enclosure _____	39-46
Shady Areas _____	47-51
Full Sun _____	52-56
Slopes and Terraces _____	57-66
Overcoming Problems _____	67-75
Pleasant Views _____	76-82
Specialty Gardens _____	83-90
Fountains/Pools/Hot Tubs _____	91-99
Specialty Structures _____	100-108
Screening _____	109-117

Part II
101 HOME LANDSCAPING DESIGNS

PART II

Using the designing and activity information in Part I, your tastes will crystallize, and you will formulate some idea of what you want in a garden. Now you can create a LERNSCAPE design that fits your personality.

The following designs represent a full spectrum of landscape possibilities. They are all done to the same scale, 1″ = 20′. Go directly to those that match your checklist responses, or browse through them and search for ideas. Note elements that reflect personal needs, such as screening, patios, entrance areas, play areas, and so on.

If one particular design is to your liking, use it as a model by which to fashion your property. Otherwise, as you thumb through the designs, mark elements that are especially appealing to you. When these general concepts are down on paper, select plants and construction materials to fit the design labels.

It's a good idea to keep the design elements simple, especially on a first attempt at design. If your design is too busy—for example, too many plant varieties, sculptural pieces or construction materials—the design may lack harmony and be confusing.

Now turn the page and LERNSCAPE your way to a personalized environment.

Scale 1″ = 20′ on All Designs

KINDERGARDENS

Swimming in Shade—Create a natural, "woodsy" landscape design, using shade tolerant shrubs and ground cover. Numerous plants will thrive in low light. Many will develop a gorgeous display of flowers and foliage.

Carefully place pool to ensure that shade trees won't rob the sun's warming rays or subject the pool to excessive falling leaves.

Patio and grill complement pool and playgym, making the perfect playground for all ages.

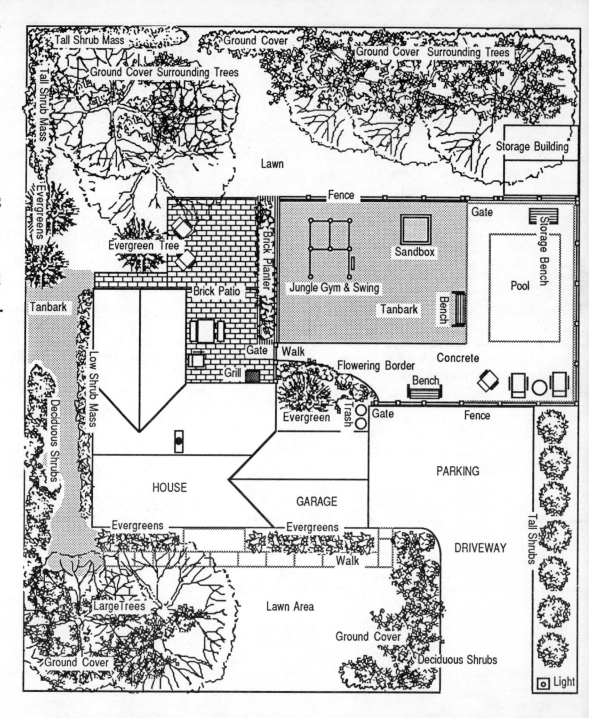

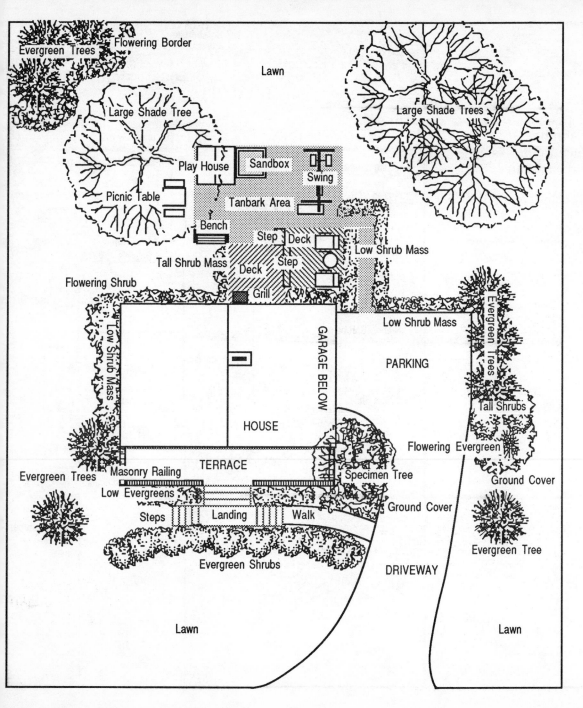

Evergreen Trees · Flowering Border
Lawn
Large Shade Tree
Large Shade Trees
Play House · Sandbox · Swing
Picnic Table
Tanbark Area
Bench
Tall Shrub Mass · Step · Deck · Low Shrub Mass
Flowering Shrub · Deck · Step
Grill
Low Shrub Mass
GARAGE BELOW
Low Shrub Mass
PARKING
Evergreen Trees
HOUSE
Tall Shrubs
TERRACE
Masonry Railing
Flowering Evergreen
Low Evergreens · Specimen Tree
Evergreen Trees · Ground Cover
Steps · Landing · Walk · Ground Cover
Evergreen Tree
Evergreen Shrubs
DRIVEWAY
Lawn
Lawn

KINDERGARDENS

Playland—The central theme of this landscape design is obviously children. From picnic to play, the attractions here are guaranteed to give mom and dad lots of time to relax on the deck, and they can still supervise with ease.

Add interest to the front of the house with an entry walk that doubles as an informal garden entrance. Evergreen trees, on the front corner, serve as a gate, through which one can meander to the rear of the property.

KINDERGARDENS

Playing in Privacy—This design emphasizes children's activities and strong spatial enclosure.

In the rear, only 35′ of fence is used to define the privacy. Spatial definition is achieved with trees, shrubs and structures. The mixture of plants and structures breaks up the rigid harsh line of a completely fenced enclosure.

The front yard is a simple and open design, purely for aesthetics.

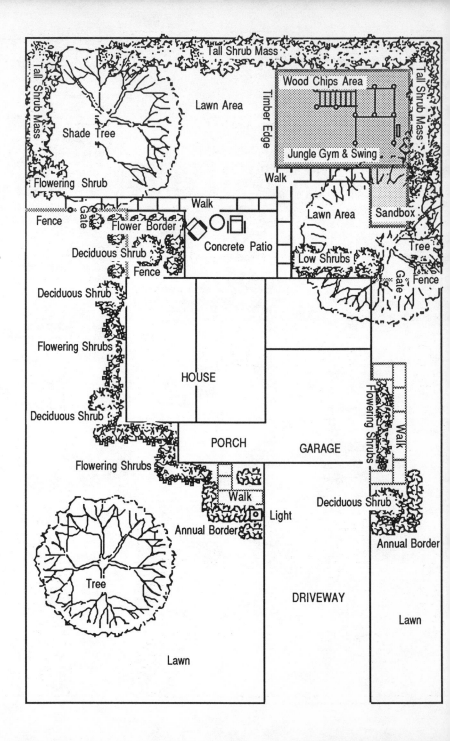

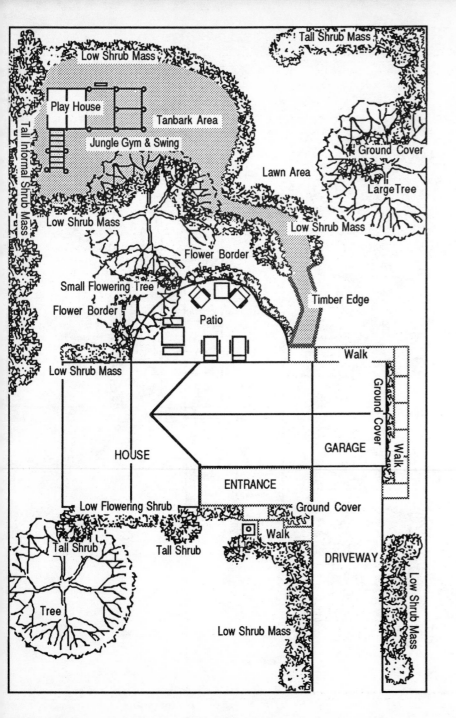

Tall Shrub Mass

Low Shrub Mass

Play House

Tanbark Area

Jungle Gym & Swing

Tall Informal Shrub Mass

Ground Cover

Lawn Area

Large Tree

Low Shrub Mass

Low Shrub Mass

Flower Border

Small Flowering Tree

Flower Border

Timber Edge

Patio

Walk

Low Shrub Mass

Ground Cover

HOUSE

GARAGE

Walk

ENTRANCE

Low Flowering Shrub

Ground Cover

Tall Shrub

Tall Shrub

Walk

DRIVEWAY

Tree

Low Shrub Mass

Low Shrub Mass

KINDERGARDENS

Child's Play—Play area, path and free-form patio lend a natural feel to this property. Natural design is very much the trend and adapts well to most terrain.

This style will work for the do-it-yourselfer. Minimal paving means that installation can be child's play.

The walkway in front, consisting of three offset, rectangular blocks, gives a contemporary look to entrance of house.

KINDERGARDENS

Function and Aesthetics—Your property should fit the surrounding landscape. Frame pleasant views, screen unpleasant ones, and leave plenty of room to play.

This design meets all of these criteria and more. Arbor, raised walk, patio, play structure, flowers, shrubs and trees create interest on the ground, vertical and overhead planes.

Play area is designed as part of the patio space. Use the same building materials for play structures and garden structures, and you will integrate the functional elements of this design with the aesthetic.

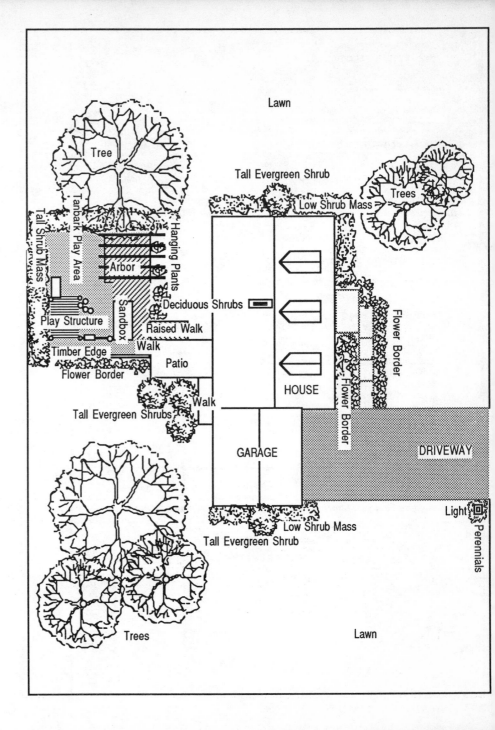

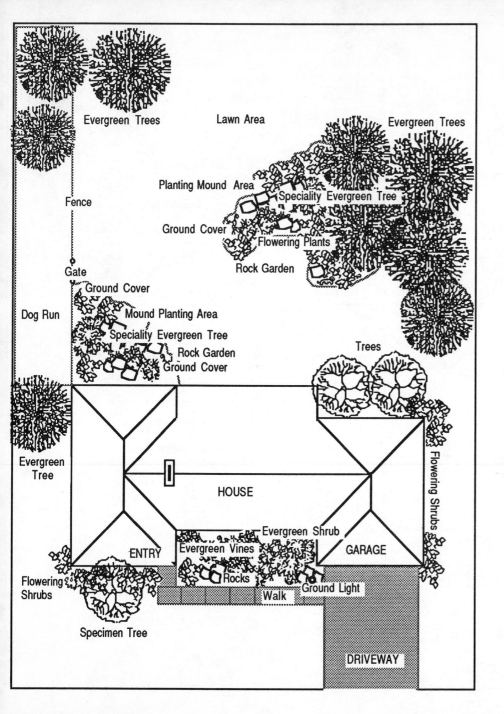

Evergreen Trees

Lawn Area

Evergreen Trees

Planting Mound Area

Speciality Evergreen Tree

Fence

Ground Cover

Flowering Plants

Gate

Rock Garden

Ground Cover

Dog Run

Mound Planting Area

Speciality Evergreen Tree

Rock Garden

Ground Cover

Trees

Evergreen Tree

HOUSE

Evergreen Shrub

Flowering Shrubs

Evergreen Vines

GARAGE

ENTRY

Rocks

Flowering Shrubs

Walk

Ground Light

Specimen Tree

DRIVEWAY

PETS

Out of the Way—Dog run placed along edge of property makes an efficient use of space. Little footage is lost and pet is out of the way, leaving a nice expanse of lawn for recreation and ease of mowing.

A mounded rock garden breaks up and partially screens the fence line. Evergreen trees to rear of fence do the same. One evergreen planted toward the front, outside the fence, hides the dog run from the street.

The massed evergreen trees give a feeling of depth to the yard and act as a backdrop for the central rock garden.

The rock garden, by the way, will certainly be easier and more pleasant to maintain, because your pet has a garden of his own.

21

PETS

Hide-a-Pet—Don't sacrifice a garden for your pet. Design a fake back on your property, much in the same way a magician uses a false bottom in a box. Install a lattice wall parallel with the property line and plant densely with vines. An overhead trellis and evergreen trees will further screen the area.

Lattice with vines is used against front wall of house to match the theme used in back. It creates an excellent narrow planting surface.

Herbs planted along the patio are in close proximity to the house for cutting. Another less obvious use is that they provide fragrance close to dog run.

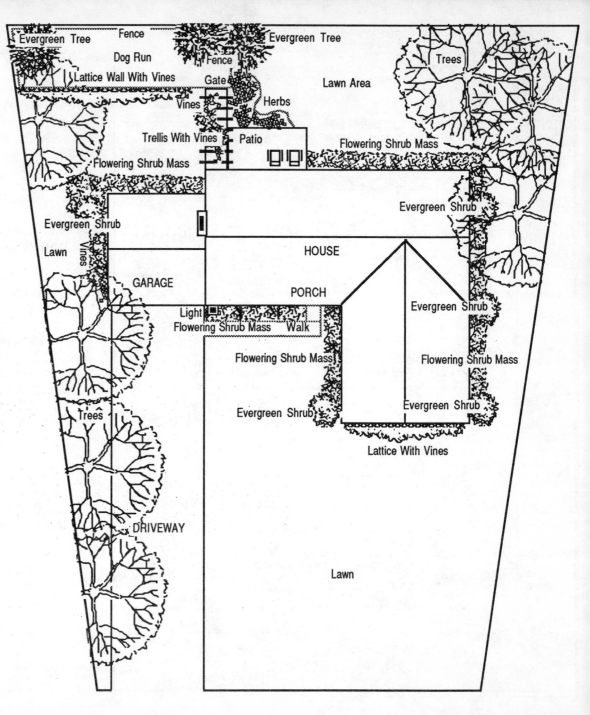

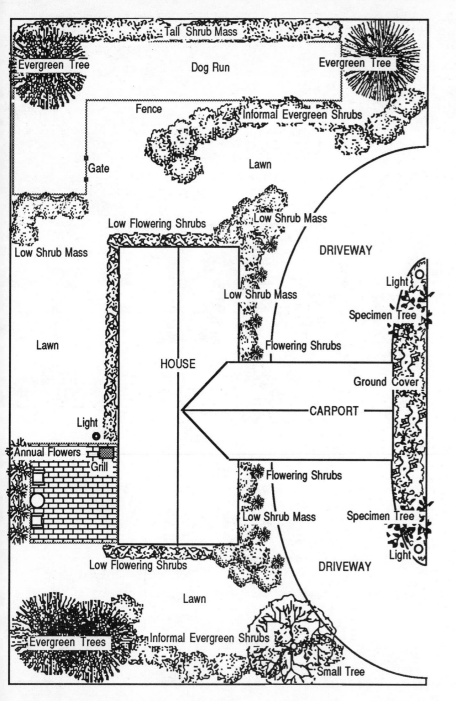

Tall Shrub Mass

Evergreen Tree

Dog Run

Evergreen Tree

Fence

Informal Evergreen Shrubs

Gate

Lawn

Low Shrub Mass

Low Flowering Shrubs

Low Shrub Mass

Low Shrub Mass

DRIVEWAY

Low Shrub Mass

Light

Specimen Tree

Lawn

Flowering Shrubs

HOUSE

Ground Cover

Light

CARPORT

Annual Flowers

Grill

Flowering Shrubs

Low Shrub Mass

Specimen Tree

Low Flowering Shrubs

Light

DRIVEWAY

Lawn

Evergreen Trees

Informal Evergreen Shrubs

Small Tree

PETS

Double Duty—Dog run is located for pet to have access to front and back of property. Shrubbery and trees are planted to hide fence enclosure, but dog will still sense if visitors are approaching. If your pet is a typical canine, he will warn residents when anyone approaches the property. Therefore, designing for your pet and property might as well include every consideration in the book, security included.

The patio has been placed away from the dog run to provide a spot for relaxing and cooking out. This design permits easy circulation around the property as well.

LOW MAINTENANCE

Tricks of the Trade—Informal shrub masses, planted with room to spread, don't require much care. Check them monthly, prune only the branches that are growing way out of proportion, and pull an occasional weed or two. The shrub mass will control most of them.

If planted with enough room to grow, evergreen trees require virtually no pruning, and with tanbark beneath, few weeds will grow. A dense ground cover is also excellent for weed control, but trim it monthly.

Keeping design elements simple (5 types of plants in entire design), thinking through the maintenance requirements before planting, and regular attention are tricks to a low-maintenance garden.

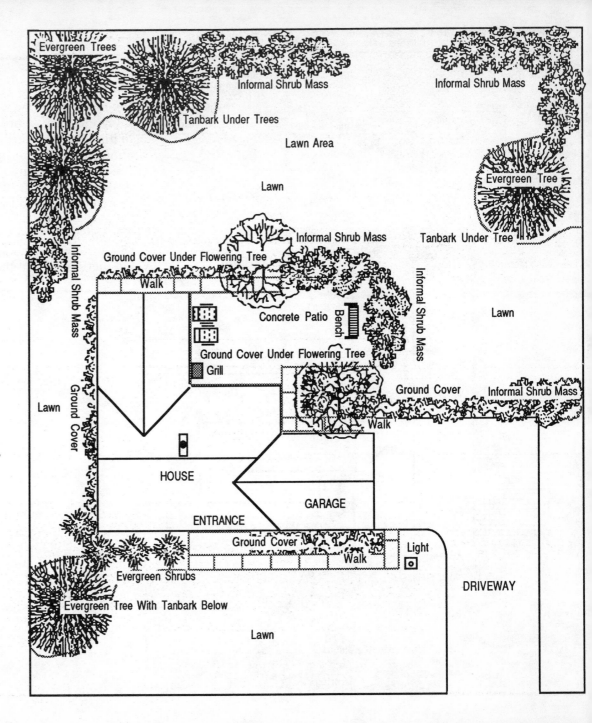

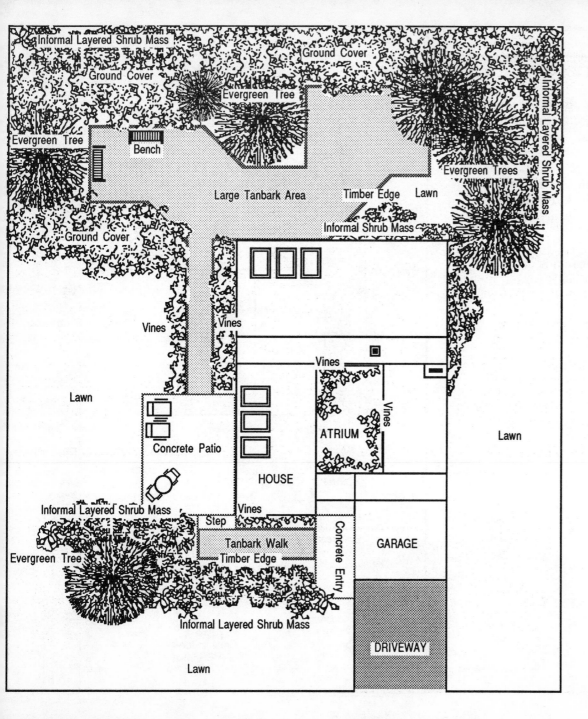

Informal Layered Shrub Mass

Ground Cover

Ground Cover

Evergreen Tree

Evergreen Tree

Bench

Evergreen Trees

Large Tanbark Area

Timber Edge

Lawn

Ground Cover

Informal Shrub Mass

Informal Layered Shrub Mass

Vines

Vines

Vines

Lawn

Concrete Patio

Vines

ATRIUM

Lawn

HOUSE

Informal Layered Shrub Mass

Vines

Step

Evergreen Tree

Tanbark Walk

Concrete Entry

GARAGE

Timber Edge

Informal Layered Shrub Mass

DRIVEWAY

Lawn

LOW MAINTENANCE

Less Lawn—Large tanbark area serves as low-cost, low-maintenance space. The geometric design and tree placement add artistic appeal.

Informal shrub masses, ground cover, patio and tanbark greatly reduce mowing area. Therefore, weekly maintenance is greatly reduced.

Don't forget to keep an eye on the rest of the property. Ground cover still needs trimming and tanbark needs freshening. If weeds become a problem, a heavy black plastic sheeting could be placed under tanbark.

LOW MAINTENANCE

Manicured and Elegant—A lawn mower and edger will keep this yard looking fit and trim. Concrete-edged bedding areas are easily maintained and have been kept manageable in size.

If time can be spent in your garden during Spring and Fall, this property would need little maintenance during the rest of the season—just soil preparation for planting flowers in Spring and clean-up in the Fall.

For the most manicured and elegant appearance, mass the same colors and similar textures together. This garden mixes low maintenance with high appeal.

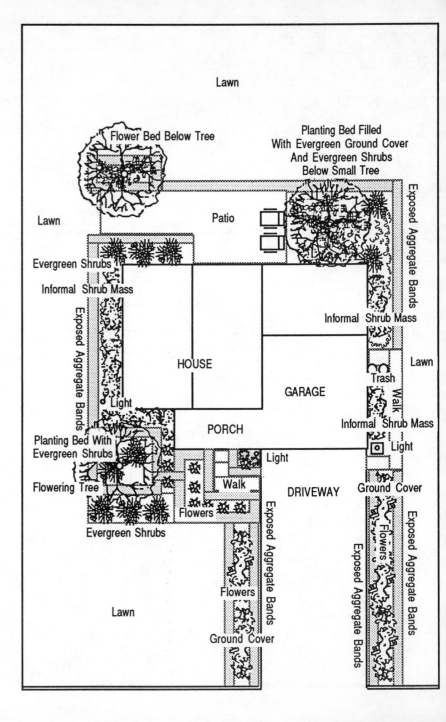

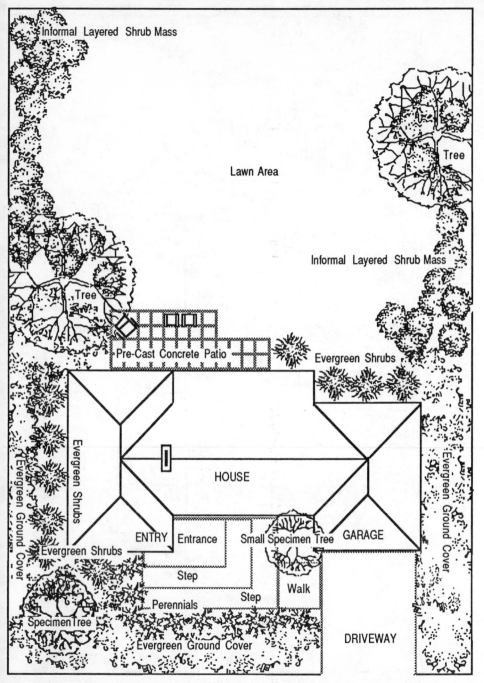

Informal Layered Shrub Mass

Tree

Lawn Area

Informal Layered Shrub Mass

Tree

Pre-Cast Concrete Patio

Evergreen Shrubs

Evergreen Shrubs

Evergreen Ground Cover

HOUSE

Evergreen Ground Cover

ENTRY   Entrance

Small Specimen Tree   GARAGE

Evergreen Shrubs

Step

Walk

Step

Specimen Tree

Perennials

DRIVEWAY

Evergreen Ground Cover

LOW MAINTENANCE

Lush and Low Maintenance—Ground cover and shrub masses confine the lawn to one area, which can be a big time saver for weekly mowing. The trees are underplanted with shrubs, reducing obstacles in the lawn.

Shrub masses can be layered, low ones in the foreground, taller ones in the background, to add interest. They should be given room to spread in order to keep a natural habitat and to require less pruning.

The ground cover will require pruning to be kept in bounds, but that's as simple as an occasional walk around the yard with a pair of electric hedge trimmers.

All in all, this design is a fairly low-maintenance proposition. You need only to know what to do and when to do it.

LOW MAINTENANCE

Natural but Controlled—Elements such as flagstone, paving, meandering bed lines and informal arrangements of shrubs should fit most any neighborhood motif. Wildflower arrangements, though, need careful planning.

There is a trend today toward landscaping with native plants. Many of these plants fall into the category of wildflowers. Wildflowers will fill an area with color, require little or no maintenance once established, and will proliferate unassisted for years to come. Unfortunately, they may become a little too prolific for the neighbors. Always create a pleasing view for all concerned.

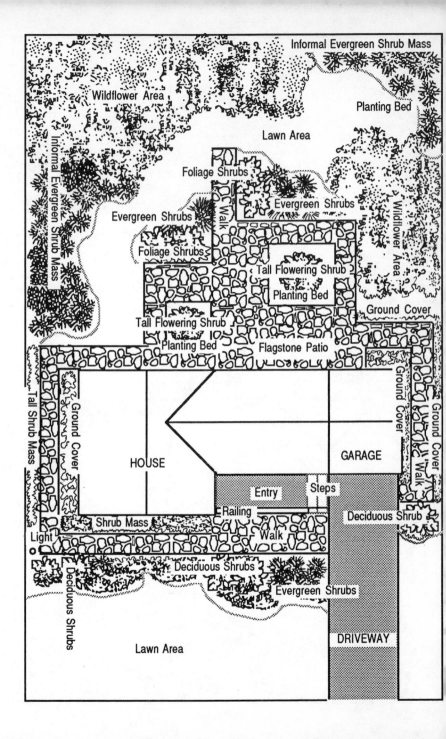

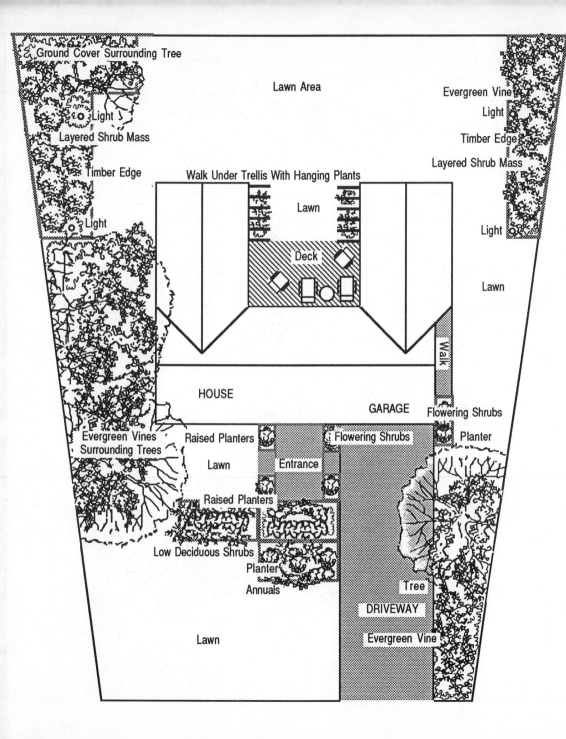

Ground Cover Surrounding Tree

Lawn Area

Evergreen Vine

Light

Layered Shrub Mass

Light

Timber Edge

Timber Edge

Layered Shrub Mass

Walk Under Trellis With Hanging Plants

Light

Lawn

Deck

Light

Lawn

Evergreen Vines Surrounding Trees

Walk

HOUSE

GARAGE

Flowering Shrubs

Raised Planters

Flowering Shrubs

Planter

Lawn

Entrance

Raised Planters

Low Deciduous Shrubs

Planter

Annuals

Tree

DRIVEWAY

Evergreen Vine

Lawn

LOW MAINTENANCE

Less Maintenance—Contrary to popular belief, less lawn does not necessarily mean less maintenance. Lawn can be some of the easiest area to care for. Shrubbery and trees need to be pruned, and beds mulched and weeded. Paving needs to be edged, shoveled (snow) and kept in good repair. All you need is a mower for a manicured lawn.

The following are several steps you can take to lower maintenance further:

Raised planters and timber edging keep bed lines straight and sharp.

Low vines or ground cover control weeds.

Hanging plants can avoid the need to dig beds by the patio or deck.

With careful planning, low maintenance can be a reality. But remember, nothing in the "built" landscape is "no maintenance."

LOW MAINTENANCE

Choosing Carefully—If you choose your plants carefully, low evergreens can be used in place of tall spreading plants. They will require much less pruning.

Small trees are easy plants to care for also. Most small trees don't need an intensive pruning program, and when they do need trimming, you can do it yourself. Many of the smaller trees have magnificent flowering qualities, and/or exfoliating colorful bark that offers a rare opportunity to introduce winter interest into your garden.

Potted plants on the entrance patio afford the opportunity to introduce color and/or exotic plants into the design. You can also plant pots with shrubs that will live outdoors year round and offer another way to create winter interest.

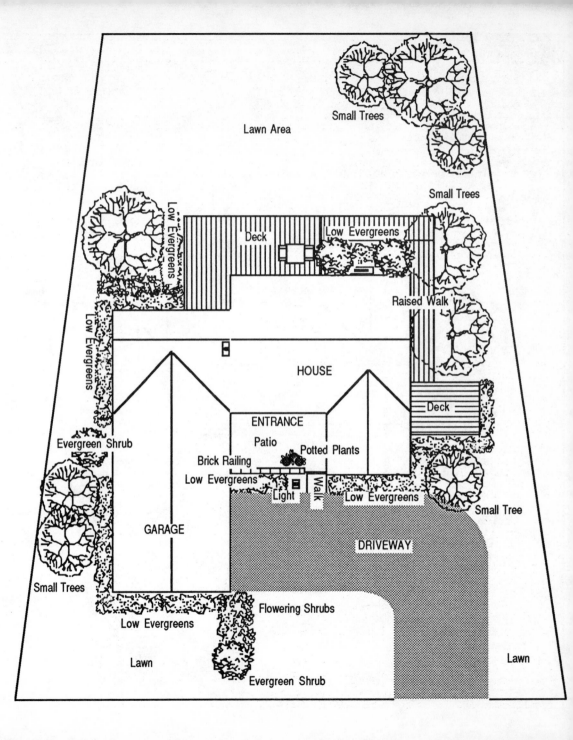

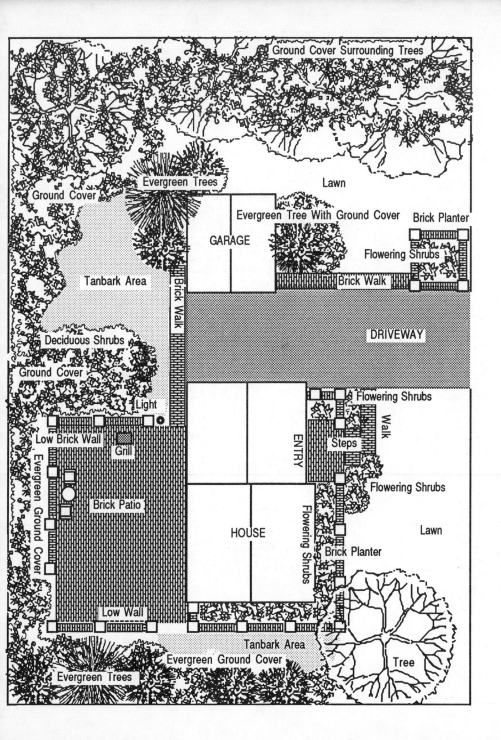

Ground Cover Surrounding Trees

Evergreen Trees

Ground Cover

Lawn

Evergreen Tree With Ground Cover

Brick Planter

GARAGE

Flowering Shrubs

Tanbark Area

Brick Walk

Brick Walk

Deciduous Shrubs

DRIVEWAY

Ground Cover

Light

Flowering Shrubs

Low Brick Wall

Walk

Grill

ENTRY

Steps

Flowering Shrubs

Brick Patio

Evergreen Ground Cover

Flowering Shrubs

HOUSE

Lawn

Flowering Shrubs

Brick Planter

Low Wall

Tanbark Area

Evergreen Ground Cover

Tree

Evergreen Trees

LOW MAINTENANCE

Majestic Air—Brick structures give the property a majestic air. You'll look forward to getting home to your castle retreat. No one will ever know that the ulterior motive of building it was to vastly reduce maintenance.

Brick patio, walks and planters will look good for many years, and they comprise a large portion of the property. Planter walls keep a good sharp line between lawn and beds. Trees and ground cover will control weeds, and tanbark creates a low maintenance play area. Tanbark also blends in well with ground cover and shrubs. These plants could encroach on the open play area without creating any maintenance problem at all.

This garden epitomizes the basic philosophy of landscape design: Manipulate the environment to create function and beauty.

STORAGE AND AESTHETICS

Practical Property—Storage shed, tucked into evergreen trees, serves as a backdrop to the deck. The overhead trellis adds an aesthetic touch, giving the shed architectural interest.

The deck is also an excellent structure to use for storage. Generally, there is a 2′ to 3′ high space under decks that could be enclosed for use with tools and equipment. It's especially good for storing longer items such as ladders and lumber.

On the garage side, a wall planted with shrubbery defines a space for trash. It would also be a good area for firewood storage.

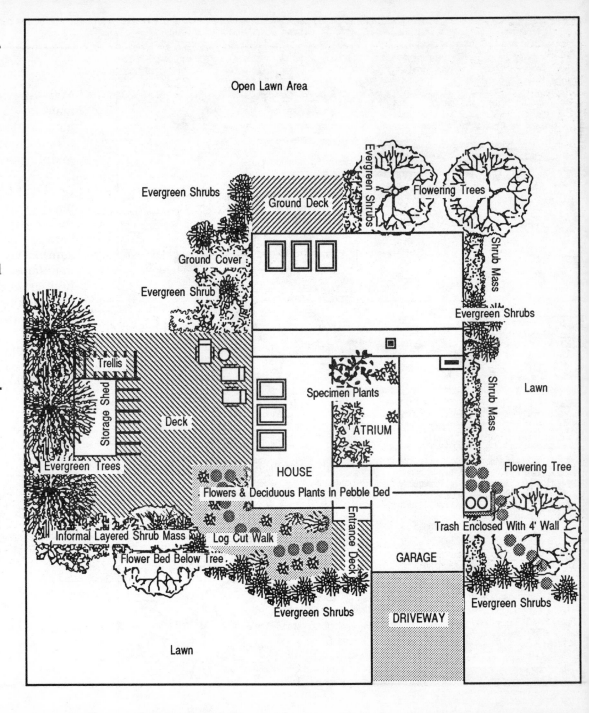

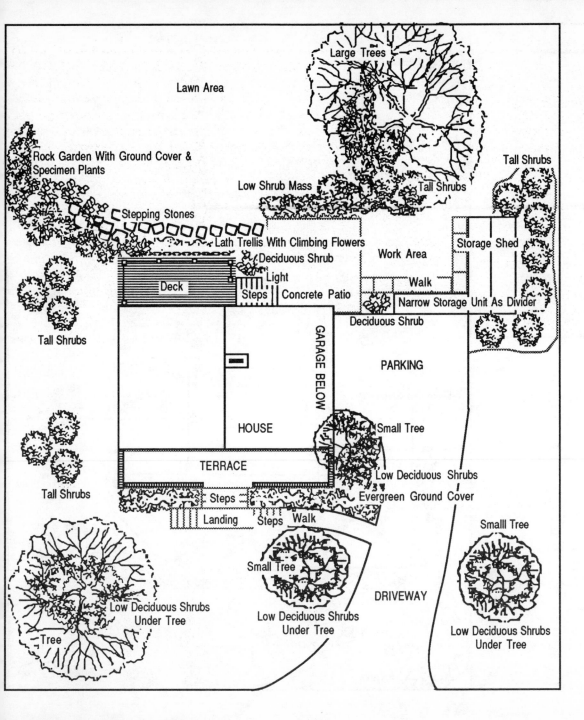

Large Trees

Lawn Area

Rock Garden With Ground Cover & Specimen Plants

Tall Shrubs

Low Shrub Mass

Tall Shrubs

Stepping Stones

Lath Trellis With Climbing Flowers

Storage Shed

Work Area

Deciduous Shrub

Light

Walk

Deck

Steps

Concrete Patio

Narrow Storage Unit As Divider

Tall Shrubs

Deciduous Shrub

GARAGE BELOW

PARKING

HOUSE

Small Tree

TERRACE

Low Deciduous Shrubs

Tall Shrubs

Steps

Evergreen Ground Cover

Landing

Steps

Walk

Smalll Tree

Small Tree

Low Deciduous Shrubs Under Tree

Low Deciduous Shrubs Under Tree

DRIVEWAY

Low Deciduous Shrubs Under Tree

Tree

STORAGE AND AESTHETICS

Multi-Functional—A narrow storage unit doubles as fence along the end of the driveway. Lath trellis doubles as storage wall along the rock garden path. A work area and shed are also provided.

The design can serve many purposes if you consider every need before the job is installed. Lots of room has been saved in this design to meet your recreational needs as well.

Large lawn, with patio and deck, offers an expanse fit for any occasion. Also, aesthetically speaking, it's well screened from the storage and work areas.

33

STORAGE AND AESTHETICS

Well Endowed—If well coordinated, many areas of the garden will be flowering throughout the growing season. Room has been provided for flowers of all sorts. Include flowers for fragrance, cutting, favorite color, length of bloom and compatibility with the design.

A storage building on the property will offer the needed space for work area, tools and fertilizer, in order to undertake your gardening activities.

You won't be at a loss for beautiful surroundings, as demonstrated by flagstone walk, patio, shade trellis, timber steps and garden path. This design has a wealth of considerations within its hedged enclosure.

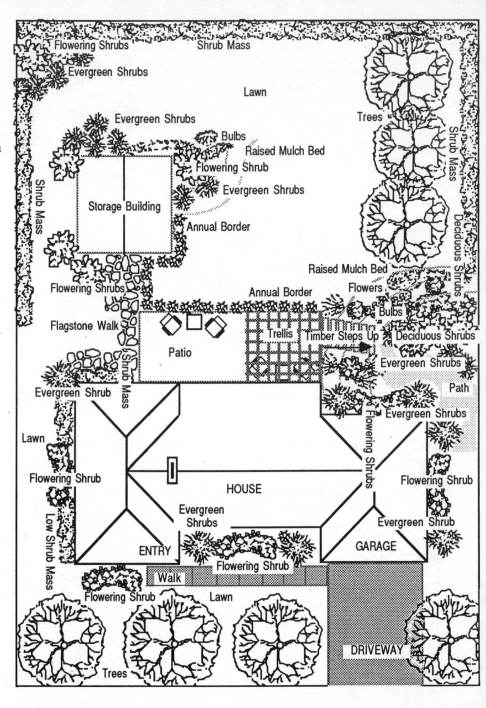

34

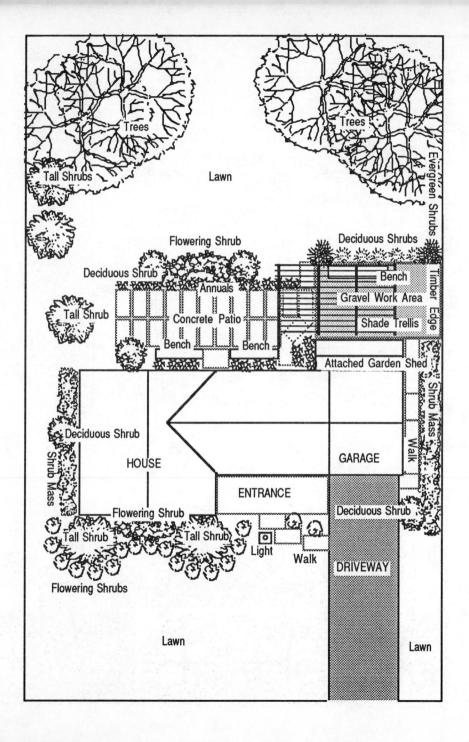

STORAGE AND AESTHETICS

Efficiency—There's only one thing you need for working in the garden, a work area. Shade trellis, bench, and a storage shed attached to garage, make inexpensive structures for working in your garden. They will also add tremendously to the looks of the patio.

Shrubbery and annuals along patio seem to take on more importance with trellised ceiling. Overhead enclosure brings the patio into people-sized proportion and makes the immediate surroundings more noticeable.

Garden location in close relationship to the house creates a smooth transition from house to patio. It's comfortable, easy to use, and adds incentive to move out of the house into the yard.

STORAGE AND AESTHETICS

Separate Splendor—What could be more aesthetically pleasing than storage space that's fenced from the main social area? Each area has its own personality. Annual flowers and vines enclose work space in flowery splendor. Entertaining area has more permanence.

Annuals around storage shed could be grown for cutting since area is fenced from visitors. Vines could also be cut for interesting stems, berries or flowers, and be used with annual arrangements.

Entertaining area has been designed with perennials and evergreens and need only be tended throughout the growing season. They'll be back the following year. Use the work area as your playground, and entertain on the patio in a garden that's coordinated for all year round.

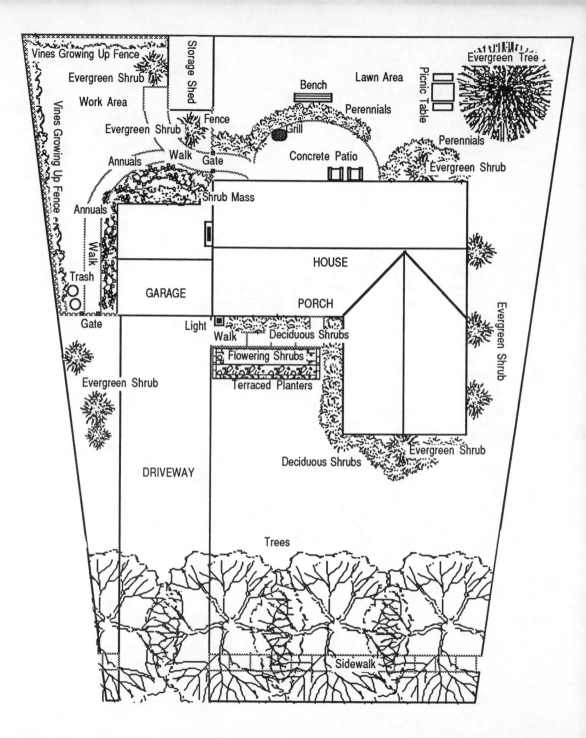

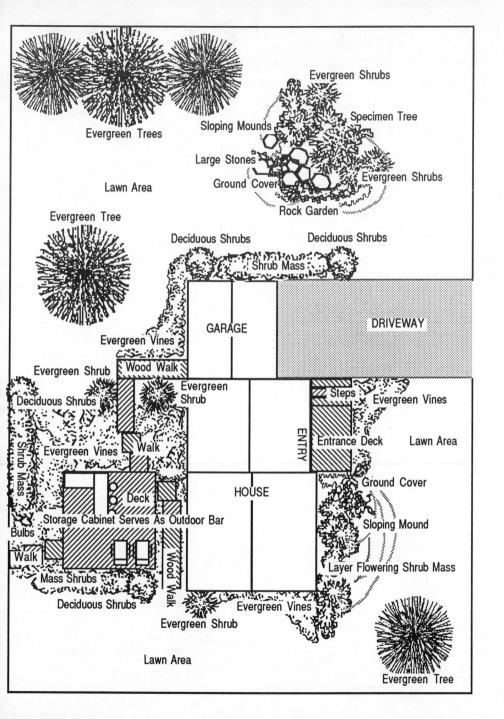

Evergreen Trees

Evergreen Shrubs

Sloping Mounds

Specimen Tree

Large Stones

Lawn Area

Ground Cover

Evergreen Shrubs

Rock Garden

Evergreen Tree

Deciduous Shrubs

Deciduous Shrubs

Shrub Mass

GARAGE

DRIVEWAY

Evergreen Vines

Evergreen Shrub

Wood Walk

Evergreen Shrub

Deciduous Shrubs

Steps

Evergreen Vines

Evergreen Vines

Walk

ENTRY

Entrance Deck

Lawn Area

Shrub Mass

Ground Cover

Deck

HOUSE

Bulbs

Storage Cabinet Serves As Outdoor Bar

Sloping Mound

Walk

Wood Walk

Mass Shrubs

Layer Flowering Shrub Mass

Deciduous Shrubs

Evergreen Vines

Evergreen Shrub

Lawn Area

Evergreen Tree

STORAGE AND AESTHETICS

Truly Tropical—Wood walk through lush greenery, amid flowering vines, blends to express a truly tropical mood.

Bar/storage cabinet combination adds to the authenticity of this arrangement. Sit on the deck and luxuriate in the foliage and feeling of the islands.

In keeping with this design motif, front entrance deck and mounded plantings should match the theme of the property. Design plantings that have large exotic foliage and flowers.

STORAGE AND AESTHETICS

Formally Inviting—Shaded deck uses storage building for privacy on one side and tall evergreens on the other. This arrangement beautifully blends storage and aesthetics in a private corner of the property.

Timber-edged gravel walk provides easy circulation to rear of house, and gravel is available in many colors and sizes. Use your favorite color and coordinate it with flowering shrubs and trees.

Entrance has been formally designed. Symmetrically balanced foundation plantings and lighting present a clean formal entry. The lawn areas in front should be meticulously cared for in order to obtain the most impressive effect from this design.

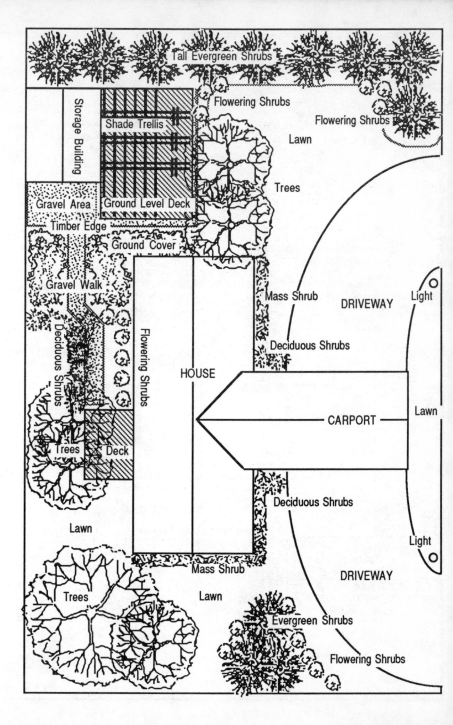

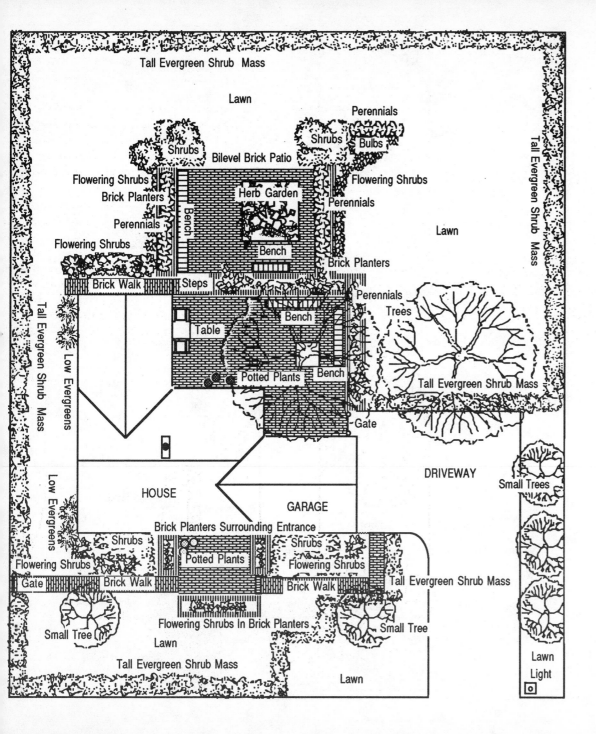

Tall Evergreen Shrub Mass

Lawn

Perennials

Shrubs

Shrubs

Bulbs

Bilevel Brick Patio

Flowering Shrubs

Flowering Shrubs

Brick Planters

Herb Garden

Perennials

Perennials

Bench

Flowering Shrubs

Bench

Brick Planters

Lawn

Brick Walk

Steps

Perennials

Table

Bench

Trees

Potted Plants

Bench

Tall Evergreen Shrub Mass

Tall Evergreen Shrub Mass

Tall Evergreen Shrub Mass

Low Evergreens

Low Evergreens

Gate

DRIVEWAY

Small Trees

HOUSE

GARAGE

Brick Planters Surrounding Entrance

Shrubs

Shrubs

Potted Plants

Flowering Shrubs

Flowering Shrubs

Tall Evergreen Shrub Mass

Gate

Brick Walk

Brick Walk

Small Tree

Flowering Shrubs In Brick Planters

Small Tree

Lawn

Tall Evergreen Shrub Mass

Lawn

Lawn Light

PRIVACY AND ENCLOSURE

Hedged In—Enclose yourself in quiet luxury. Make the surroundings spacious, while insisting upon your privacy. A tall evergreen shrub mass around the property can imply strong separation between you and the world outside. A gate will offer a peek at the garden for those who pass by. What a treat!

In back, a bilevel brick patio offers two separate "courtyard gardens"—one for socializing, which creates a smooth outdoor/indoor relationship, and one to sit in and enjoy the fragrant plants and flowers that add to this pleasant arrangement.

PRIVACY AND ENCLOSURE

Composite of Small Spaces—Some of the finest gardens in the world are simply composites of many smaller gardens. This design incorporates the finest of them. Rounded patio garden, entrance courtyard garden, atrium garden, and beautifully enclosed utilitarian garden blend to give the picture of a home that has been tastefully designed for beauty and enclosure.

The use of a fence is an excellent way to create enclosure, but it's an element that shouldn't be overdone in the landscape. Here, fence and utility structures are used only where needed, and harsh straight lines are softened by greenery in a variety of sizes and shapes.

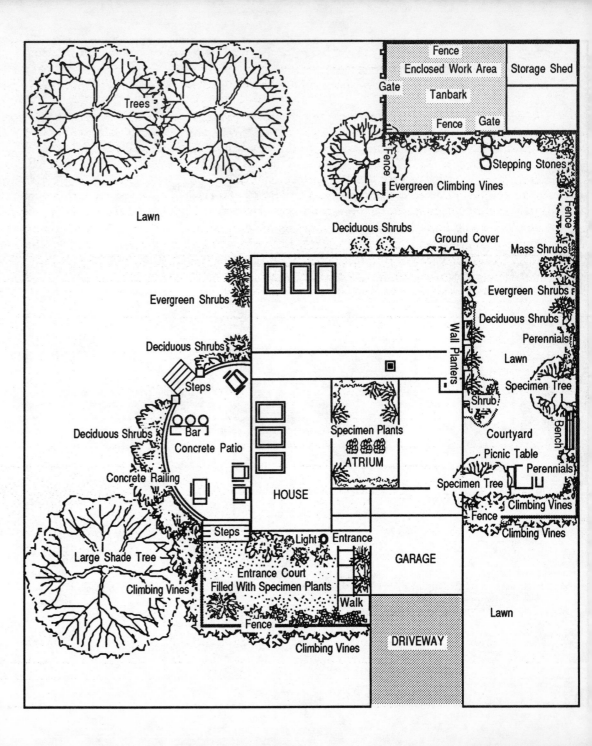

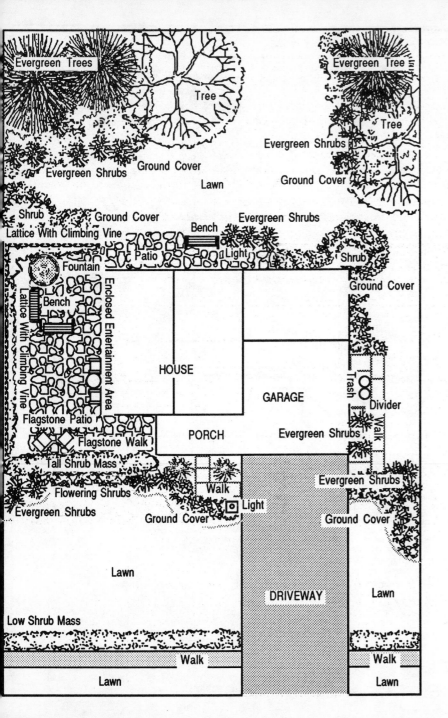

PRIVACY AND ENCLOSURE

Wraparound Patio—With every turn you'll view changes. Few landscape features, carefully placed, can offer many differing moods and ambiances.

Notice how benches are placed to offer a maximum of seating and a variety of views with a minimum number of seats. View the fountain garden in latticed privacy, or turn to socialize with guests.

For a stronger sense of privacy, sit in rear yard within sight and earshot of fountain, while islands of greenery offer wooded views for meditation.

PRIVACY AND ENCLOSURE

An Exclusive Touch—A high brick wall brings house out to garden, creating the appearance of a larger house. This tall, free-standing structure makes a strong statement of enclosure, but in the rear, the wall's open-ended design provides a view of the ornamentally planted entryway.

Move outside this courtyard and behold another garden. This one comes complete with seating and perennial garden. For an extra bonus, shade trees on the hottest side of the house can save fuel dollars as well.

The entry welcomes visitors with flowering shrubs, perennials and privacy, lending an exclusive touch to this property.

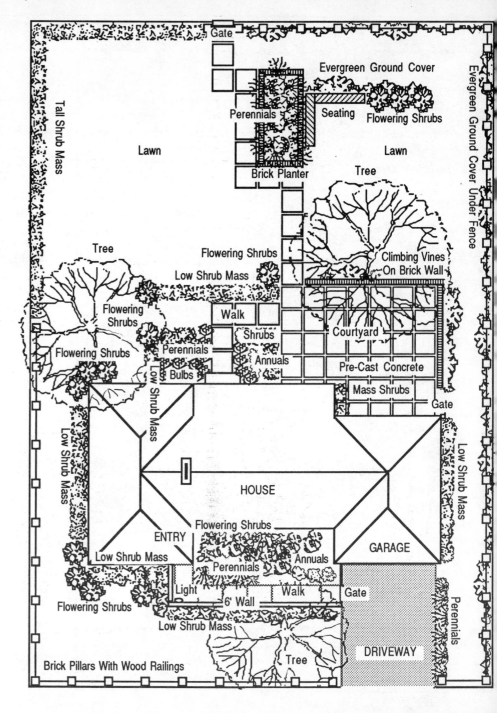

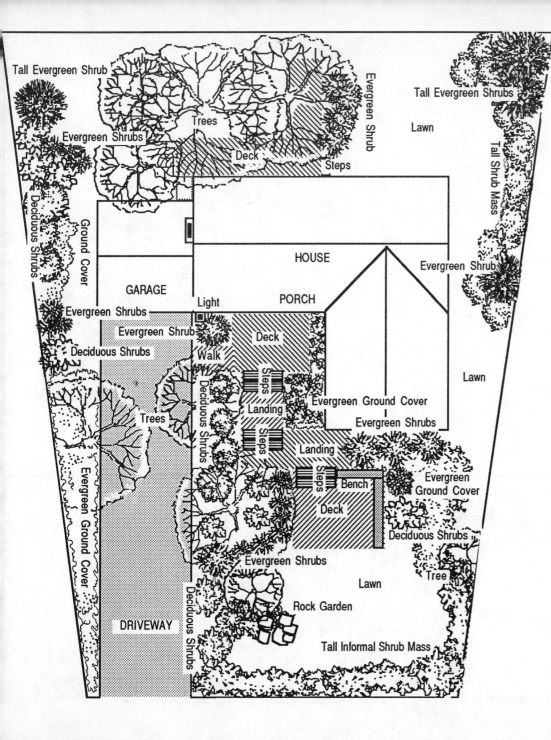

Tall Evergreen Shrub

Evergreen Shrubs

Trees

Deck

Tall Evergreen Shrubs

Lawn

Evergreen Shrub

Steps

Tall Shrub Mass

Deciduous Shrubs

Ground Cover

HOUSE

Evergreen Shrub

GARAGE

Light

PORCH

Evergreen Shrubs

Evergreen Shrub

Deck

Deciduous Shrubs

Walk

Steps

Trees

Landing

Deciduous Shrubs

Steps

Evergreen Ground Cover

Evergreen Shrubs

Lawn

Landing

Steps

Bench

Evergreen Ground Cover

Deck

Deciduous Shrubs

Evergreen Ground Cover

Evergreen Shrubs

Lawn

Tree

Deciduous Shrubs

Rock Garden

DRIVEWAY

Tall Informal Shrub Mass

PRIVACY AND ENCLOSURE

Tastefully Informal—A front yard with lots of room can be fun. Stepped decks take you down into a garden that couldn't be further removed from yet in closer proximity to the house. Informal shrub masses define the garden, set off the house, screen the property and offer lots of interest as you move down to the rock garden.

L-shaped deck in the rear gives a usable outdoor area close to house for utility, or perhaps for brunch or tea in the afternoon.

This design is a tastefully informal arrangement. It exemplifies the creation of privacy without the need for fences or hedge rows.

PRIVACY AND ENCLOSURE

Personal Touches—With the personal touches in this landscape design, it will appear that your garden is the reason that you own the home. The outdoor bar offers one type of entertaining. The intimate space in the dimly lit rear deck offers another type. Shrubs and trees are designed for you to get the maximum effect from both areas.

One can also tell that you were smart enough to have a say in the design of the driveway. Rather than settling for the standard 10′ width, it's wide enough to turn around in. If you used a paving material with texture and interest, the effect would be quite handsome as well.

Now find trees, shrubs and flowers to complete this picture of your personality.

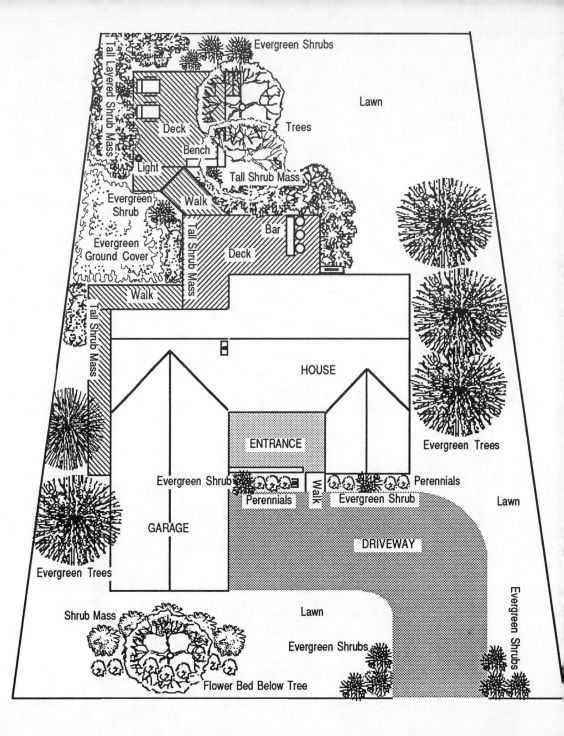

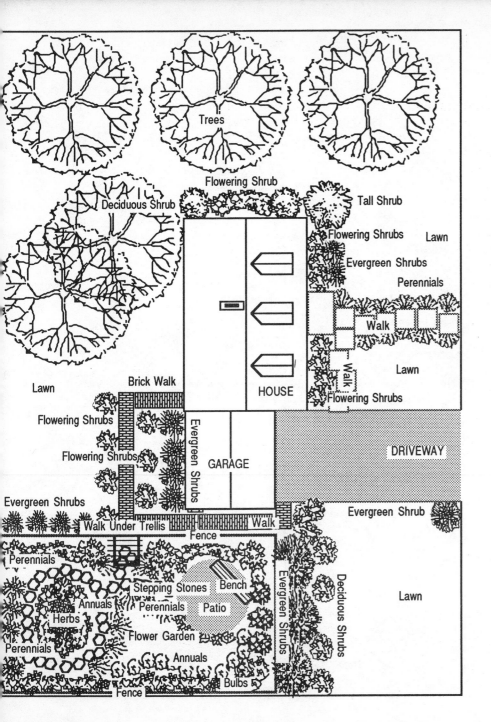

Trees

Flowering Shrub

Deciduous Shrub

Tall Shrub

Flowering Shrubs

Lawn

Evergreen Shrubs

Perennials

Walk

Lawn

Lawn

Brick Walk

Evergreen Shrubs

HOUSE

Walk

Flowering Shrubs

Flowering Shrubs

Flowering Shrubs

Evergreen Shrubs

GARAGE

DRIVEWAY

Evergreen Shrubs

Evergreen Shrub

Walk Under Trellis

Walk

Fence

Perennials

Stepping Stones

Bench

Evergreen Shrubs

Deciduous Shrubs

Lawn

Annuals

Perennials

Patio

Herbs

Flower Garden

Perennials

Annuals

Bulbs

Fence

PRIVACY AND ENCLOSURE

Just Right—Design is challenging when the house fits on your land so that the property is wider than it is long, but you can still have an expanse of treed lawn as well as a spacious private garden. The placement of the garden is what achieves this.

What a perfect arrangement this would be if the pleasant view from the house was toward the trees and, at the same time, the unpleasant view was beyond the fenced garden. The trees also add balance to the design and would provide cooling summer shade without shading the herbs and flowers in the private garden.

Walks are arranged in a very practical fashion, offering circulation from house to garden. Walkway is placed sensibly in front in order to access house from the street and driveway. Although walks meander, the user can follow a straight line from one point to the other.

PRIVACY AND ENCLOSURE

Progressive Realization—The practice demonstrated here is called progressive realization, and does it ever add interest to a garden! Plants and paths are designed so that as you move through the garden you don't see everything all at once. Instead, you get hints of what lies beyond.

This causes the viewer to walk on and see what lies ahead. It also offers a variety of small enclosed areas in which to relax. Each area has a quality and personality of its own.

When entering the property from the front, a centrally located driveway allows partially screened views of the rear garden. Trees and islands of greenery balance the house on the property, lending an overall feeling of comfort and stability.

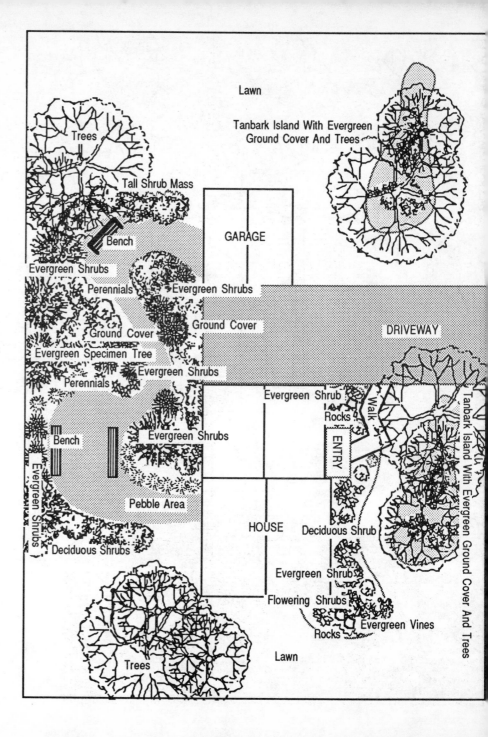

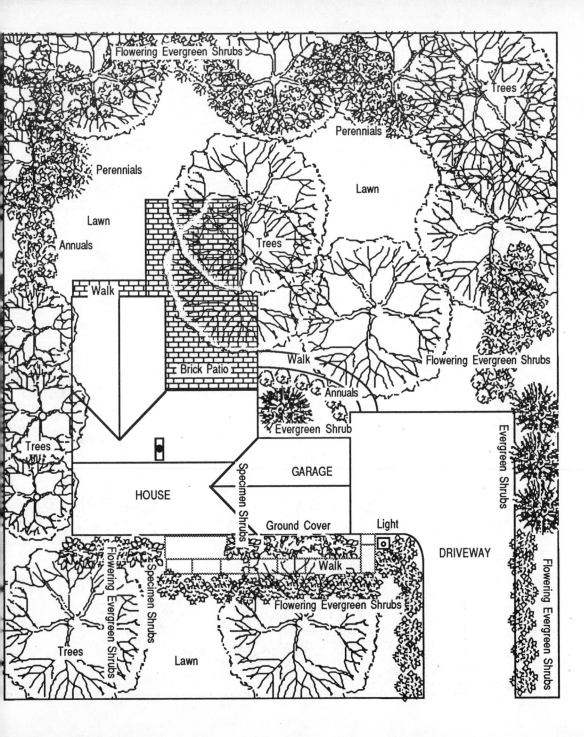

Flowering Evergreen Shrubs

Trees

Perennials

Perennials

Lawn

Lawn

Annuals

Trees

Walk

Brick Patio

Walk

Trees

Annuals

Flowering Evergreen Shrubs

Evergreen Shrub

GARAGE

Specimen Shrubs

HOUSE

Ground Cover

Light

DRIVEWAY

Specimen Shrubs

Flowering Evergreen Shrubs

Walk

Trees

Flowering Evergreen Shrubs

Lawn

Evergreen Shrubs

Flowering Evergreen Shrubs

SHADY AREAS

Inspirational—Trees are nature's canopy. They are the easiest and most effective way of designing for the overhead plane. When trees are used, a property of this size will be scaled more to people proportion. The effect that is achieved is suggestive of a cathedral, with pillars and ceiling of your design and nature's construction.

Considerations for choosing the trees are the habit or shape, mature size, fall color and a non-invasive root system.

Use shade-tolerant plants when choosing the shrubs. Beautiful flowering evergreens that work perfectly in shadier locations are available, and they maintain a wall of greenery throughout the year.

SHADY AREAS

Inviting Enclosure—When you are surrounded by shade trees, a sense of strong enclosure is implied, but the views aren't impeded in the least. By keeping the limbs elevated, trees will frame pleasant vistas, setting off the house, yard and properties beyond. The house will not hold moisture and mildew if trees are placed far enough away, but will still offer cooling summer shade.

Evergreen ground cover gives a lusher carpet than lawn in strong shade, and you can choose one that has flowering value as well. The ground cover will also match the textures of the trees, creating a very nice complement on the ground plane.

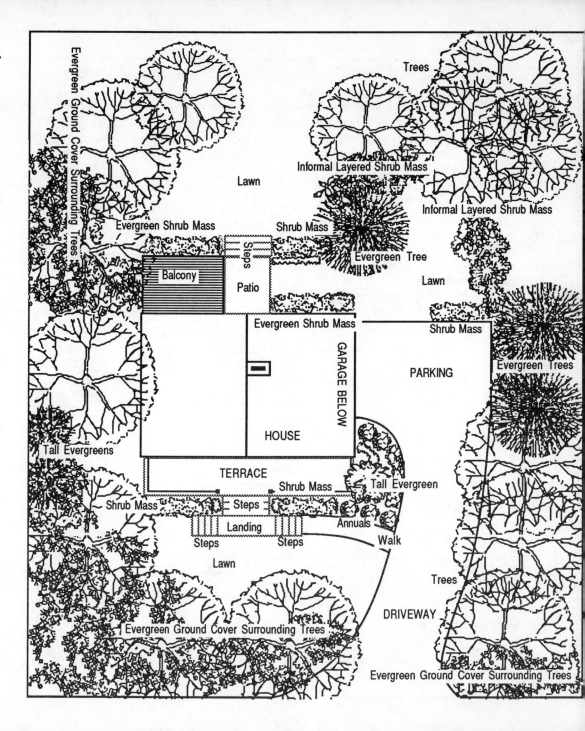

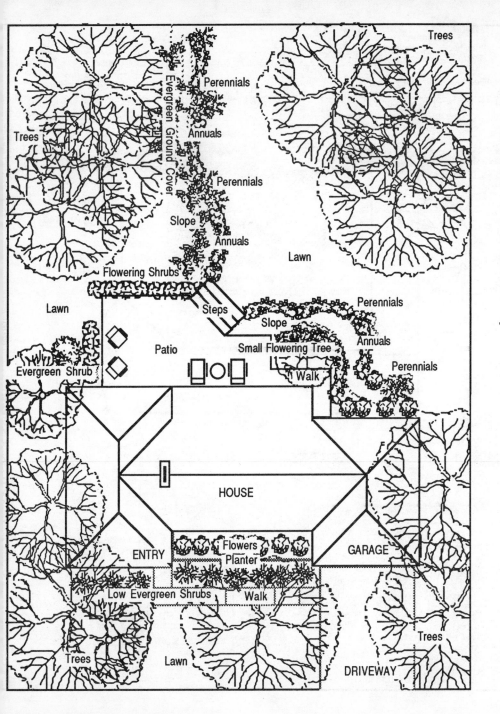

Trees

Perennials

Annuals

Perennials

Evergreen Ground Cover

Slope

Annuals

Flowering Shrubs

Lawn

Lawn

Steps

Slope

Perennials

Patio

Small Flowering Tree

Annuals

Evergreen Shrub

Walk

Perennials

HOUSE

Flowers
Planter

ENTRY

GARAGE

Low Evergreen Shrubs

Walk

Trees

Lawn

Trees

DRIVEWAY

SHADY AREAS

Carefully Maintained—Patio and flower beds create the focal point of this property. Lawn and trees set off the flowered patio, but trees must be carefully placed and maintained so not to shade the flowers. Choose trees carefully as well to ensure that the lawn will thrive underneath them.

Use shade-tolerant grass seed and shrubs. Keep trees clean of dead wood and crossing branches, and prune the lower limbs in order to help keep the landscaping in top condition for many years to come. Don't forget to fertilize and weed. That always yields your best bottom line.

49

SHADY AREAS

Paved in the Shade—Plants and soil won't withstand foot traffic, especially in shady areas. Patios offer usable space without negatively impacting the environment.

In front, a brick entry and patio lends a formal feeling and will fit nicely into the yard. This patio is a necessity if you wish to use this shady space.

Concrete is the most practical low-maintenance material for patios, but large expanses of it can be harsh in appearance. Soften its effect by adding other elements. In the rear, a deck planted with a specimen tree and a vine-covered lattice wall are used.

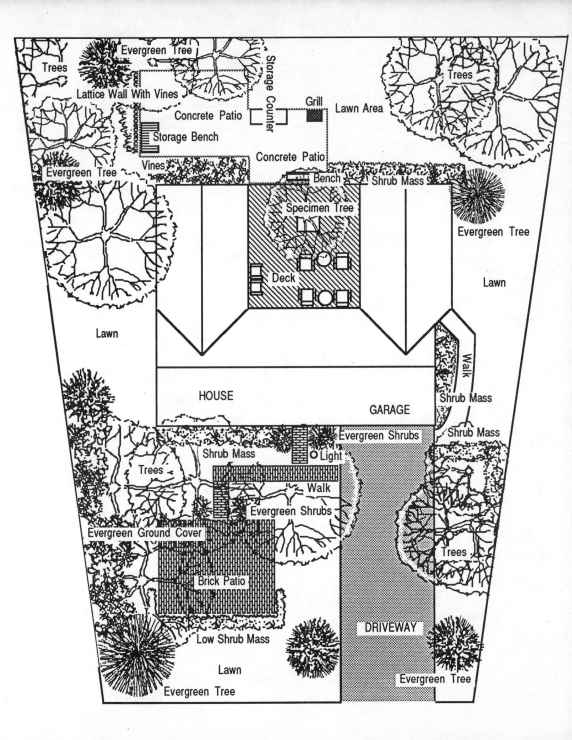

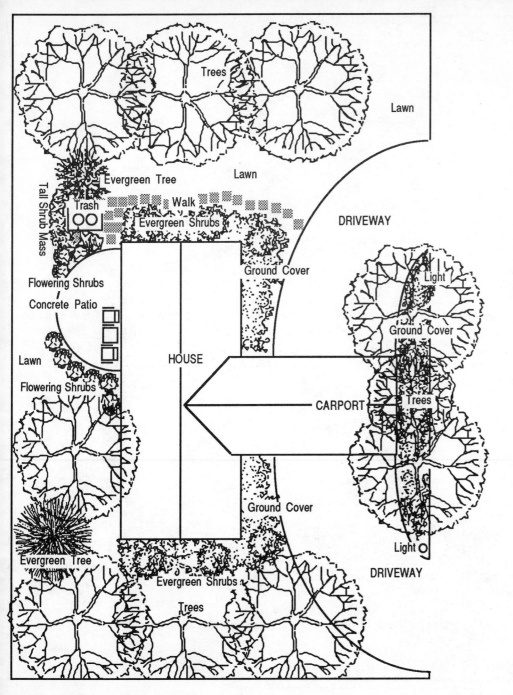

Trees

Lawn

Lawn

Evergreen Tree

Tall Shrub Mass

Trash

Walk

Evergreen Shrubs

DRIVEWAY

Flowering Shrubs

Concrete Patio

Ground Cover

Light

Lawn

Ground Cover

HOUSE

Flowering Shrubs

CARPORT

Trees

Ground Cover

Evergreen Tree

Light

Evergreen Shrubs

DRIVEWAY

Trees

SHADY AREAS

Trees, Trees, Trees—Tree-lined property and semicircular driveway give an estate-like character and continuity to this wide, shallow lot. Although there are many practical reasons for using trees in the landscape, the aesthetics of this design far outweigh the practical value.

Trees create cooling shade and can lessen energy consumption, but those benefits are secondary to the interest that they can offer. Trees should be chosen to complement the roof line, set off or frame the lower plantings, and of course, produce an exciting fall display. They shouldn't hide the house.

A variety of shrubs (flowering and/or evergreen) will soften the sharp 90° angle of the house. Remember to mass similar textures, and when plants of the same variety are massed, use all the same color.

FULL SUN

Simple Solution—Trees aren't the only way to achieve outdoor shade. Perhaps shade trees don't grow well where you live, or maybe you're a sun worshipper and don't want them. A little shade is always nice to have, and a vine-covered walk-under trellis is a perfect way to achieve it. The shade trellis is a lot less competitive with the other plants and won't ever overgrow its bounds or require expensive tree work. It provides a simple solution to add a touch of shade.

Take full advantage of both the sunshine and the protected shade spots. In making use of these two areas, you should be able to grow almost any plant your heart desires. Play around with a variety of plants over a period of time to determine the best ones for you. The use of flowers makes playing around affordable.

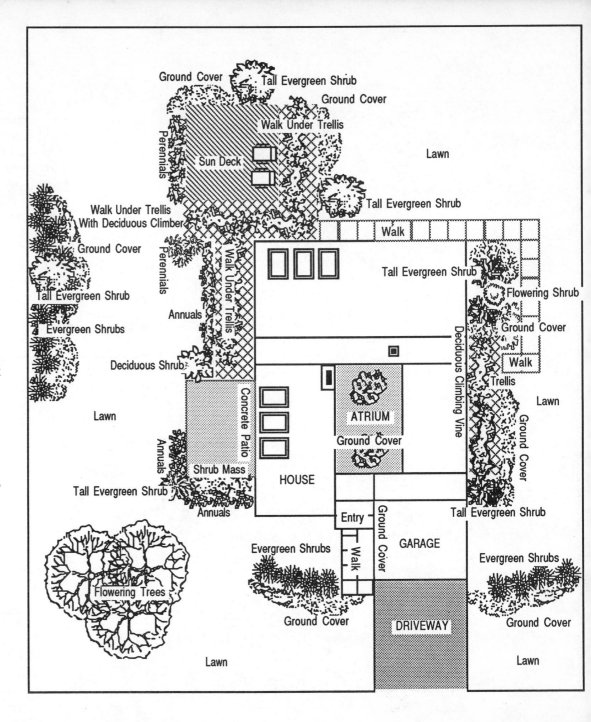

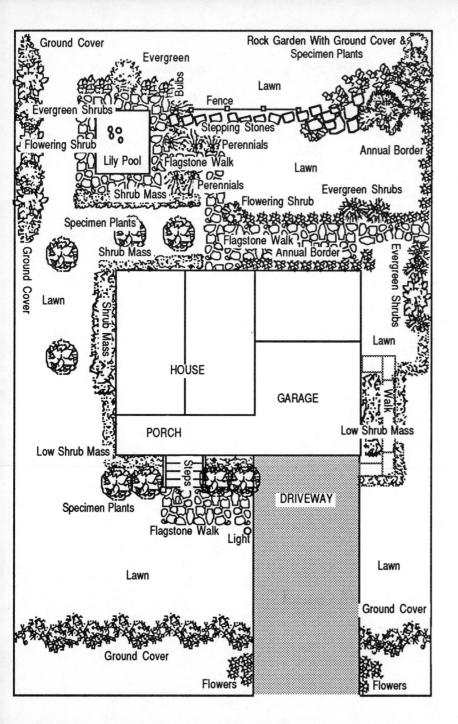

Ground Cover

Evergreen

Rock Garden With Ground Cover & Specimen Plants

Evergreen Shrubs

Bulbs

Fence

Lawn

Stepping Stones

Flowering Shrub

Perennials

Annual Border

Lily Pool

Flagstone Walk

Lawn

Perennials

Shrub Mass

Flowering Shrub

Evergreen Shrubs

Specimen Plants

Flagstone Walk

Shrub Mass

Annual Border

Ground Cover

Lawn

Shrub Mass

Evergreen Shrubs

Lawn

Walk

HOUSE

GARAGE

Low Shrub Mass

Low Shrub Mass

PORCH

Steps

Specimen Plants

DRIVEWAY

Flagstone Walk

Light

Lawn

Lawn

Ground Cover

Ground Cover

Flowers

Flowers

FULL SUN

Adding Interest—Take advantage of full sun. Both features in this yard do best in it. Rock garden and lily pool thrive better and attain their full capability when located in a sunny spot.

Rock gardens, which feature heaths, heathers, herbs, dwarf conifers and specimen trees, are generally more prolific in full sun. Sun also affords the opportunity for one to choose from a wide variety of plants.

A lily pool makes a fine complement to the garden. Fish and plants can be put in the water together to attain an almost perfect balance. The pool will need little maintenance. Another advantage of a pool is that it adds sound, touch, movement, color and light reflection to the garden.

FULL SUN

Inanimate Objects—Sometimes trees won't thrive because the soil conditions or climate are too extreme. Design with that in mind and use plants which thrive in barren situations (there are many).

Also design with non-living elements. Use rocks to build a specimen bed and create a focal point in front. Use paths of log rounds for circulation.

If that's not enough, add a terraced wall in front to create a sunny courtyard. It protects the plants inside from the harsh drying winds of winter and sun in summer, and it serves as a support for vines, introducing a lush flowering, vertical element to the front yard.

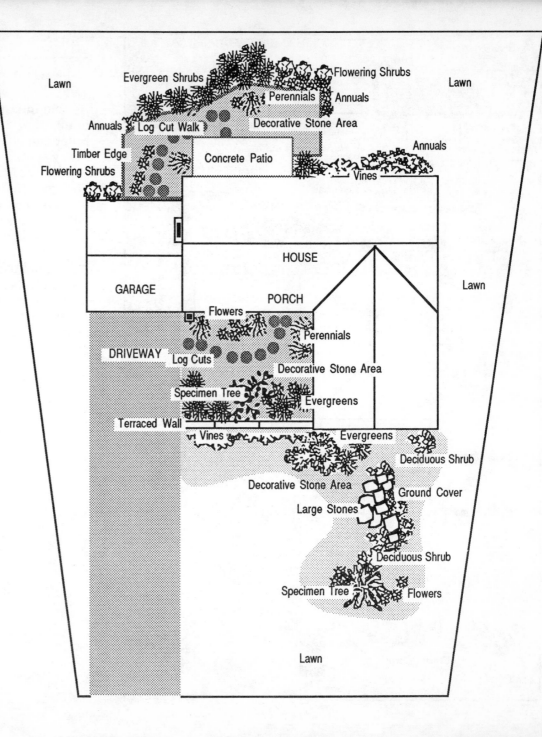

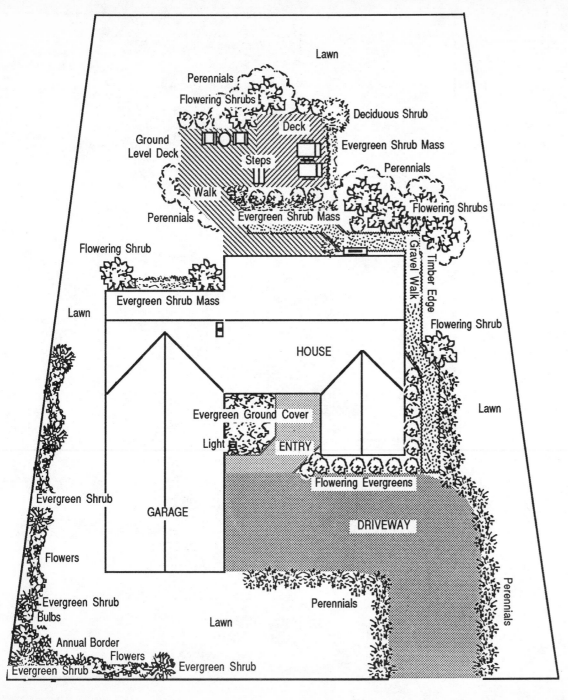

Lawn

Perennials

Flowering Shrubs

Deciduous Shrub

Deck

Ground Level Deck

Evergreen Shrub Mass

Steps

Perennials

Walk

Evergreen Shrub Mass

Perennials

Flowering Shrubs

Evergreen Shrub Mass

Flowering Shrub

Gravel Walk

Timber Edge

Evergreen Shrub Mass

Lawn

Flowering Shrub

HOUSE

Lawn

Evergreen Ground Cover

Light

ENTRY

Flowering Evergreens

Evergreen Shrub

GARAGE

DRIVEWAY

Flowers

Evergreen Shrub

Bulbs

Perennials

Annual Border

Lawn

Perennials

Flowers

Evergreen Shrub

Evergreen Shrub

FULL SUN

High Light/Low Maintenance—The largest variety of plant materials available to gardeners are those that thrive in full sun. Unfortunately the largest group of weeds are also those that thrive in full sun. The simple plantings in this design keep down on the maintenance of the beds. Flowers keep up the looks.

A perennial border along the paved areas comes back every year to soften the lines of the paving. It can be mowed down annually, as it loses ornamental value, and be back stronger than ever in several months.

In the rear, the decks provide sunny outdoor living spaces with good accessibility from house and front driveway. Surround decks with flowers, and give yourself the incentive to use the decks for entertaining and for basking in the sun.

FULL SUN

Taking Care of Itself—Full sun is the lifeblood of many living organisms. Without it, life becomes sparse, pale, and then non-existent. Most animals need protection from the hottest sun, but most plants thrive on it (if you remember to water). Especially effective in these conditions are fruits and flowers.

A wide selection of berry bushes is available that will quickly naturalize and create shrub masses. All you need to do is pick the berries and prune to keep in bounds.

Wildflowers can be seeded for the initial planting. Most will continue to replenish themselves year after year. Choose wildflowers carefully and they could be a valuable adjunct to the property by offering fragrance, spices, color and fresh and dried cut flower arrangements.

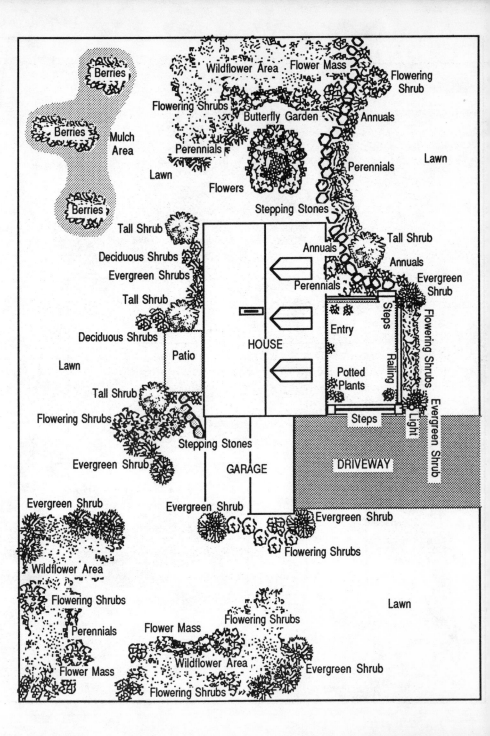

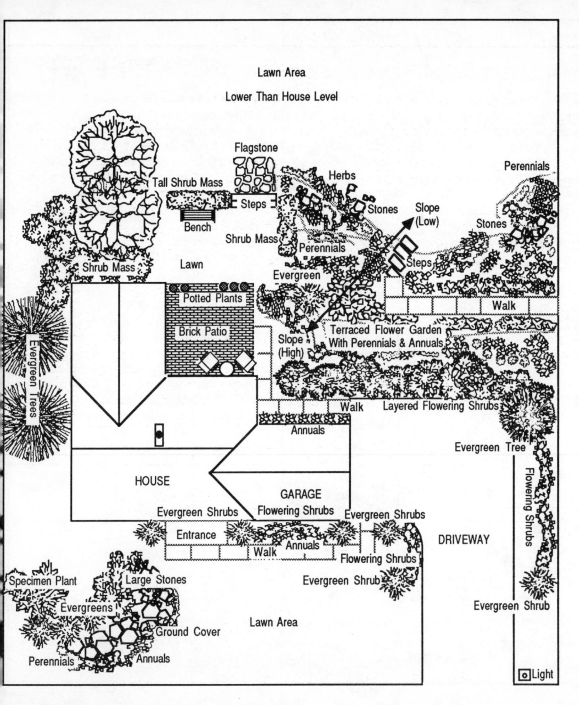

Lawn Area

Lower Than House Level

Flagstone

Herbs

Perennials

Tall Shrub Mass

Steps

Stones

Slope (Low)

Stones

Bench

Shrub Mass

Perennials

Lawn

Steps

Shrub Mass

Evergreen

Potted Plants

Brick Patio

Slope (High)

Terraced Flower Garden With Perennials & Annuals

Walk

Walk

Layered Flowering Shrubs

Annuals

Evergreen Tree

Evergreen Trees

HOUSE

GARAGE

Flowering Shrubs

Flowering Shrubs

Evergreen Shrubs

Evergreen Shrubs

Entrance

Annuals

Walk

DRIVEWAY

Flowering Shrubs

Shrub Mass

Specimen Plant

Large Stones

Evergreen Shrub

Evergreens

Evergreen Shrub

Ground Cover

Lawn Area

Perennials

Annuals

🔲Light

SLOPES AND TERRACES

Scenic Overlook—Large banked area off the rear of the house is usually considered to be a problem. Here, the slope is necessary in order to create this extremely attractive terrace garden.

Get a valley or glen effect from the level changes. Plant with layered masses of shrubbery, annuals and perennials. Create a natural rock outcropping and a stepped walk through the garden. Be sure to thickly plant the bank to avoid weeding or mowing.

In front, use stone outcropping, and set off stones by backplanting them with evergreens. A tall pine specimen growing up from the lower evergreens carries this theme into the vertical plane.

57

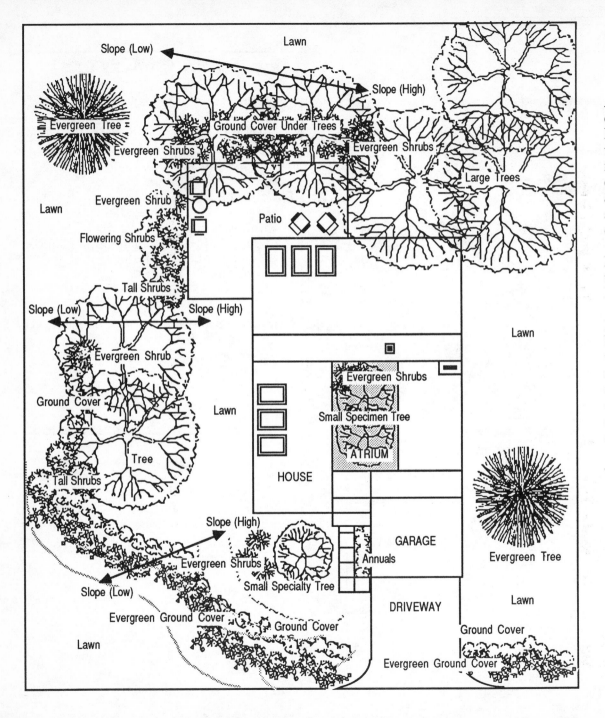

Slope (Low)
Lawn
Slope (High)
Evergreen Tree
Ground Cover Under Trees
Evergreen Shrubs
Evergreen Shrubs
Large Trees
Lawn
Evergreen Shrub
Patio
Flowering Shrubs
Tall Shrubs
Slope (Low)
Slope (High)
Lawn
Evergreen Shrub
Ground Cover
Lawn
Evergreen Shrubs
Small Specimen Tree
ATRIUM
Tree
HOUSE
Tall Shrubs
GARAGE
Slope (High)
Evergreen Tree
Evergreen Shrubs
Small Specialty Tree
Annuals
Slope (Low)
DRIVEWAY
Evergreen Ground Cover
Ground Cover
Lawn
Lawn
Ground Cover
Evergreen Ground Cover

SLOPES AND TERRACES

Air of Importance—Slopes are made to order for the contemporary look of this home. Ground-covered banks flowing up to the house give it a clear look of importance. Use a small tree, with especially interesting characteristics, and a specimen evergreen tree as sculptural pieces on each side of the entrance.

In the atrium, plant the same specialty tree and evergreen shrubs to mirror the look in the front yard.

Lawn-covered banks in rear form the back part of this pedestal, which gives the house its air of importance. The informal row of shade trees planted along the rear adds to the energy efficiency of this modern home, and offers a back drop, which the house appears to be tucked into.

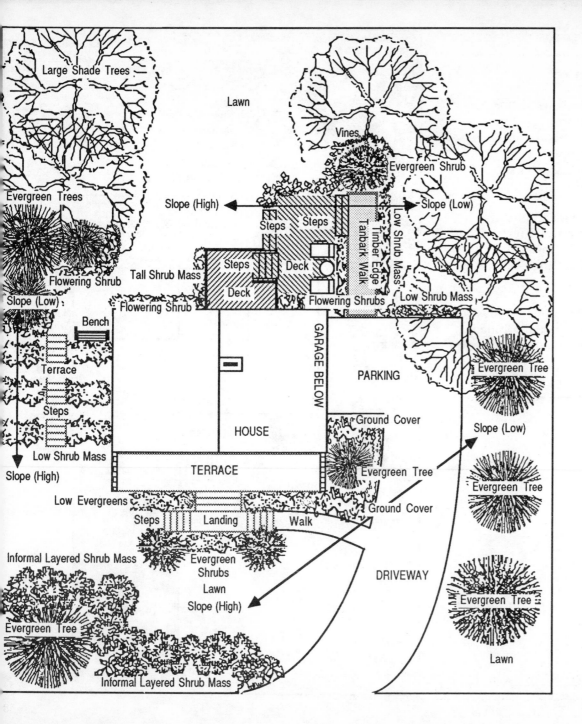

Large Shade Trees

Lawn

Vines

Evergreen Shrub

Evergreen Trees

Slope (High)

Slope (Low)

Low Shrub Mass

Steps

Steps

Timber Edge
Tanbark Walk

Deck

Flowering Shrub

Steps

Steps

Deck

Low Shrub Mass

Slope (Low)

Tall Shrub Mass

Deck

Flowering Shrubs

Flowering Shrub

Bench

GARAGE BELOW

PARKING

Evergreen Tree

Terrace

Ground Cover

Slope (Low)

Steps

HOUSE

Evergreen Tree

Evergreen Tree

Low Shrub Mass

TERRACE

Slope (High)

Ground Cover

Low Evergreens

Evergreen Tree

Steps

Landing

Walk

Informal Layered Shrub Mass

Evergreen
Shrubs

DRIVEWAY

Lawn

Evergreen Tree

Slope (High)

Evergreen Tree

Informal Layered Shrub Mass

Lawn

SLOPES AND TERRACES

American Renaissance—Driveway and entrances lead visitors into lower level. Guests are greeted on terrace or lower rear deck. From there visitors can move into the main house and entertaining areas.

This treatment very closely resembles principles applied to Italian Renaissance gardens of the 16th and 17th centuries. The reason for designing in this manner is the same today as it was then. The area was very hilly, which necessitated including slopes into the design.

The upper yard, with bench, also mimics the Italian design. Some estates would have an upper natural area above the house to use for walks and hunts. Although we may walk, we won't hunt on most of our properties today, nor would it be practical to copy the priceless sculptures and grand water displays used in gardens of that period. For most of us, the terraced gardens and lawns of the American Renaissance period will have to suffice.

SLOPES AND TERRACES

Disguised—Slopes can create problem drainage patterns, which in this case, have been improved by means of a drainage channel through the back yard. This design uses the channel as a stream, and it comes complete with stones along the bank, a footbridge and shrubs massed to soften the edge.

This is a similar treatment to the landscape architecture found in parks. Drainage is worked in as a water feature, and benches are tucked into lush plantings. The result is a purely aesthetic, nonutilitarian, peaceful setting—an excellent disguise.

The deck and rock garden by the house are oriented toward the water feature, but porch and plantings partially hide it. By blocking the view in this manner, you've added interest and a reason to move out into the garden.

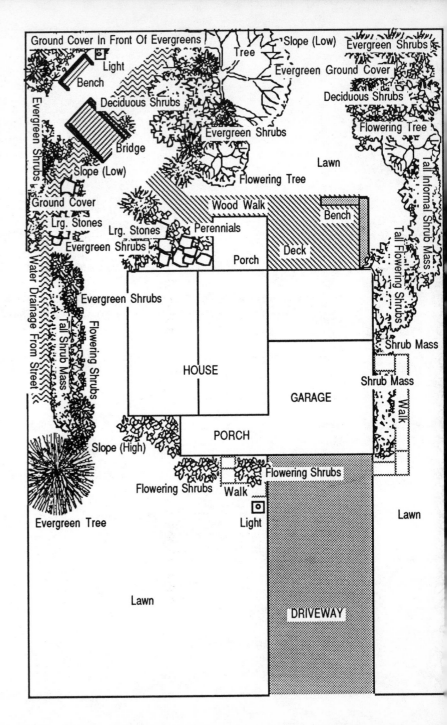

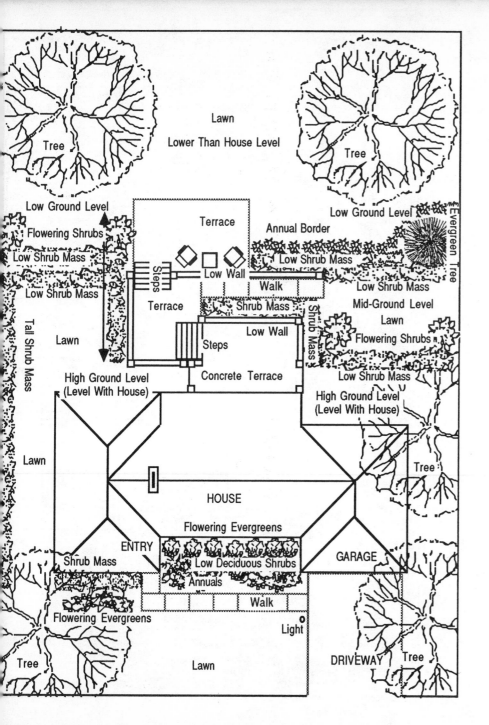

Lawn
Lower Than House Level

Tree

Tree

Low Ground Level

Low Ground Level

Evergreen Tree

Flowering Shrubs

Terrace

Annual Border

Low Shrub Mass

Low Shrub Mass

Low Wall

Steps

Low Shrub Mass

Walk

Low Shrub Mass

Low Shrub Mass

Terrace

Shrub Mass

Mid-Ground Level

Low Wall

Lawn

Tall Shrub Mass

Lawn

Steps

Flowering Shrubs

Shrub Mass

High Ground Level
(Level With House)

Concrete Terrace

Low Shrub Mass

Lawn

High Ground Level
(Level With House)

Tree

HOUSE

Flowering Evergreens

ENTRY

GARAGE

Shrub Mass

Low Deciduous Shrubs

Annuals

Flowering Evergreens

Walk

Light

Tree

Lawn

DRIVEWAY

Tree

SLOPES AND TERRACES

Formally Fashioned—House, lawn and terraces are squared on the property. Rows of shrubs grace the upper edge of the back yard where property begins to slope downward. The effect is very formal.

Tri-level terraces afford the opportunity to view the garden from many perspectives. The downward slope of the property lends a spacious touch for people standing on the deck. A pleasant view beyond the back of the property would be magnificent from the terrace.

The formal effect is carried throughout the design by a tall hedge row on the left and four shade trees symmetrically balanced on the four corners of the property.

SLOPES AND TERRACES

Mountain Living—The mountain home is in. Make the most of it by integrating your property into the environment. Use plants that are native to the area, or match the surrounding flora.

Design a series of steps and exposed aggregate landings to lead up to your mountain retreat and a patio that's situated in a comfortable spot. In this hemisphere the most pleasant orientation is to the southeast with shading to the southwest.

Several other suggestions if you're new to mountain living are: screen the prevailing winds in winter, channel them for coolness in summer, understand your property's drainage pattern and make sure the basement stays dry during highest water table. The time to make these considerations, by the way, is when your foundation is dry.

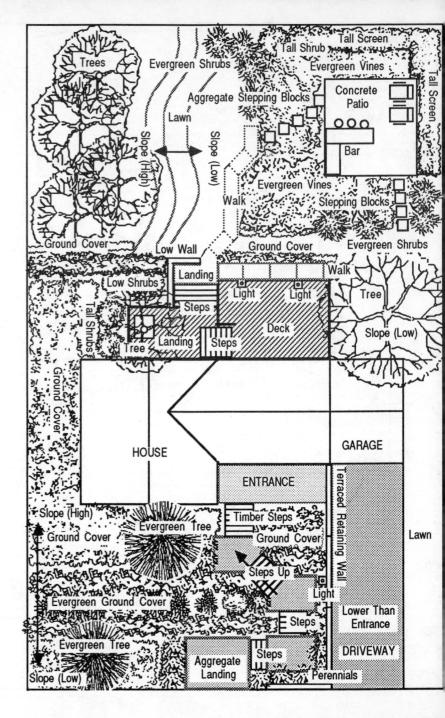

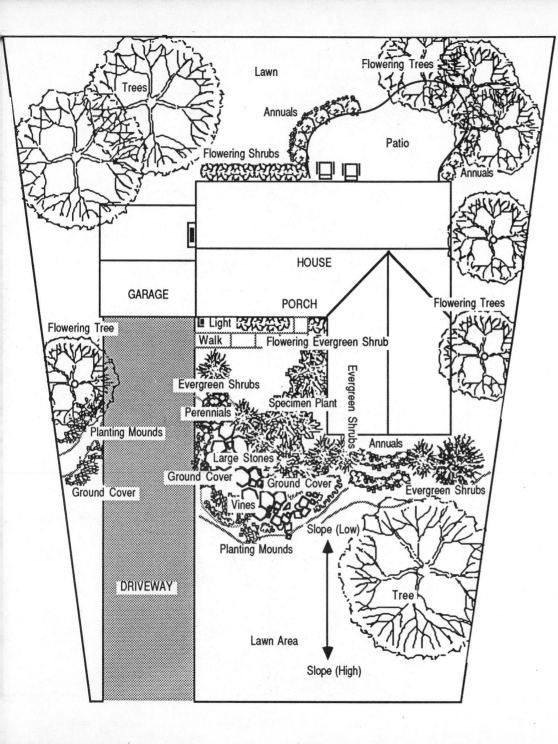

Lawn

Trees

Flowering Trees

Annuals

Patio

Flowering Shrubs

Annuals

HOUSE

GARAGE

PORCH

Flowering Trees

Flowering Tree

Light

Walk

Flowering Evergreen Shrub

Evergreen Shrubs

Evergreen Shrubs

Perennials

Specimen Plant

Planting Mounds

Annuals

Large Stones

Ground Cover

Ground Cover

Evergreen Shrubs

Ground Cover

Vines

Slope (Low)

Planting Mounds

Tree

DRIVEWAY

Lawn Area

Slope (High)

SLOPES AND TERRACES

Inward Orientation—One of the warmest, homiest locations for your house is a site nestled down in a hollow. The front slope and rock arrangement (which was probably dug from the property) help to achieve this inward orientation.

Hopefully the slope is mowable. Plants other than lawn would work to cover the front bank but most would take much longer to establish, and maintenance of this area would be somewhat more difficult.

Flowering trees around the property take the place of shrubs. Fewer trees than shrubs are needed to create a large mass. In front, only one flowering tree is needed on the planting mound to define the property line along driveway.

SLOPES AND TERRACES

A Lot of Living Room—A series of retaining walls move user and eye gently through the back terraced flower garden. Beyond the flower garden is a vine-covered secret garden where you can read and relax the afternoon away.

Above these gardens are decks that command a view of the stepped flower arrangements and vine-covered pergola. The wraparound deck/balcony/raised boardwalk combination could conceivably get more use than the house in warmer climes. Entrance deck placed just off driveway offers garden visitors an entry directly into the back yard.

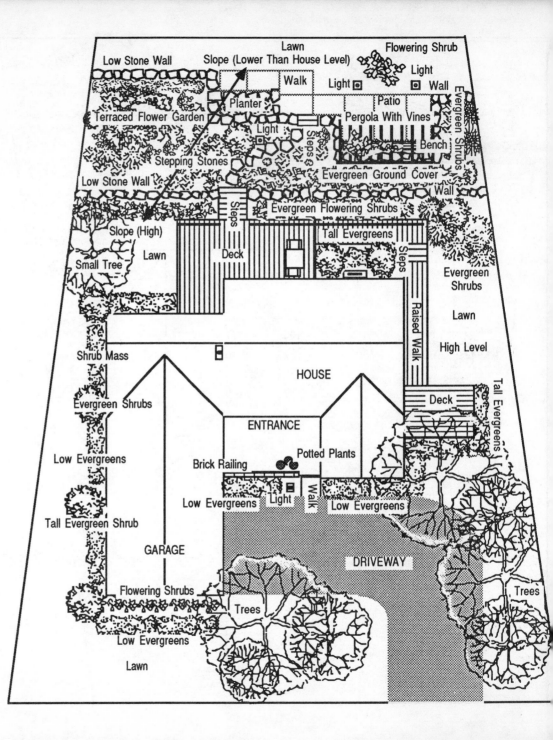

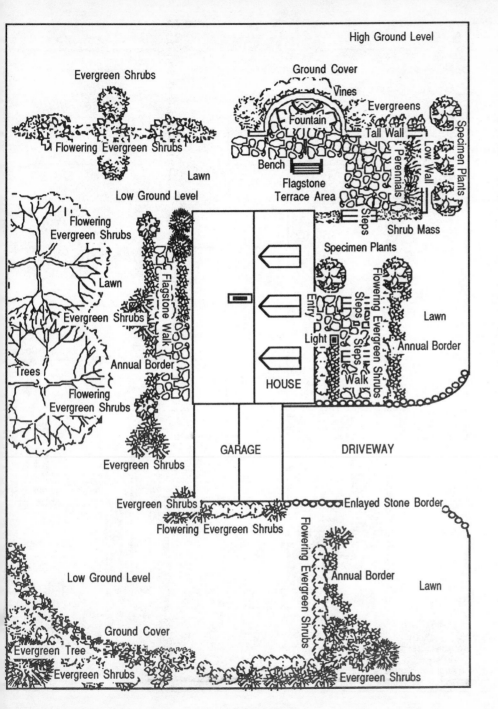

High Ground Level

Evergreen Shrubs

Ground Cover

Vines

Evergreens

Flowering Evergreen Shrubs

Fountain

Tall Wall

Bench

Low Wall

Perennials

Specimen Plants

Low Ground Level

Lawn

Flagstone Terrace Area

Flowering Evergreen Shrubs

Steps

Shrub Mass

Lawn

Specimen Plants

Flowering Evergreen Shrubs

Flagstone Walk

Evergreen Shrubs

Entry

Steps

Lawn

Trees

Annual Border

Light

Steps

Annual Border

Flowering Evergreen Shrubs

Walk

HOUSE

Evergreen Shrubs

GARAGE

DRIVEWAY

Evergreen Shrubs

Enlayed Stone Border

Flowering Evergreen Shrubs

Flowering Evergreen Shrubs

Low Ground Level

Annual Border

Lawn

Ground Cover

Evergreen Tree

Evergreen Shrubs

Evergreen Shrubs

SLOPES AND TERRACES

Jolly Old England—Representative of the English natural garden period, this design would complement a house built of any material, but its effect with a house constructed of stone would be tremendous.

The obvious focal point of this garden is the vine-covered fountain and amphitheater structure. The structure also serves as a retaining wall, creating a level terrace and main patio area.

Plants during the English natural period were allowed to grow in a natural fashion. Curves and flowing lines were used, and naturalized flowers had great appeal.

This design offers you the opportunity to apply these principles. Seize the opportunity, but make it fit your personality.

SLOPES AND TERRACES

Sunken Garden—With terraced planters, sloped driveway and beds of mixed ground cover, the entire property becomes a sunken garden. Ground covered bank and terraced planters become strong vertical elements as you move down the driveway into the garden. This vertical enclosure is further emphasized by the house and garage walls.

Moving into the front entrance strengthens enclosure so user experiences the full impact of being surrounded by greenery and flowers. Viewer can also enter into rear garden by way of a path that is graced with tall trees and flowers. Upon entering the back garden, the orientation is more outward. Therefore the distant view again becomes important.

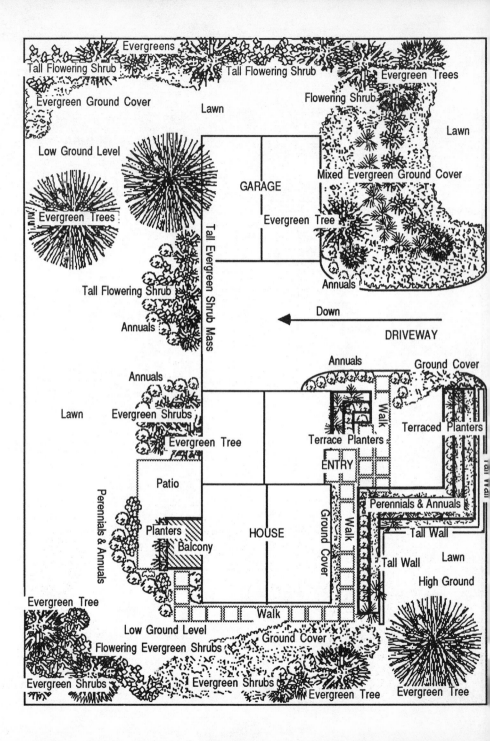

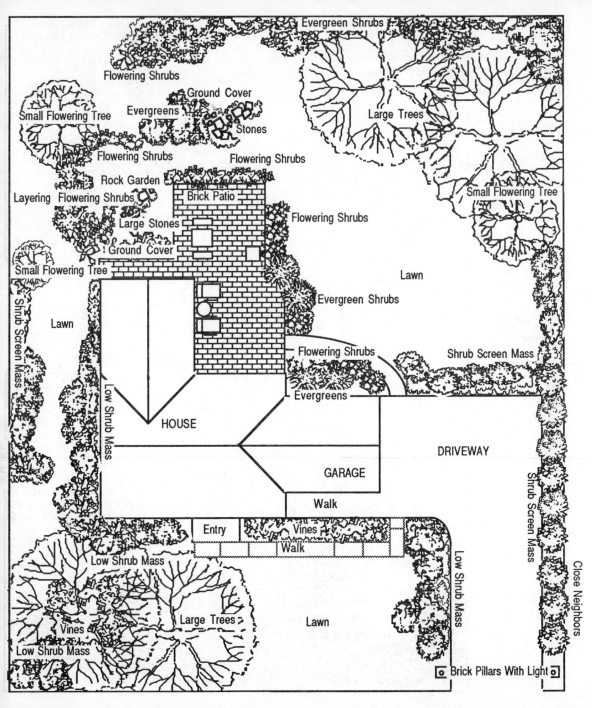

Evergreen Shrubs

Flowering Shrubs

Small Flowering Tree

Ground Cover

Evergreens

Stones

Large Trees

Flowering Shrubs

Flowering Shrubs

Small Flowering Tree

Rock Garden

Layering Flowering Shrubs

Brick Patio

Flowering Shrubs

Large Stones

Ground Cover

Small Flowering Tree

Evergreen Shrubs

Lawn

Lawn

Shrub Screen Mass

Shrub Screen Mass

Flowering Shrubs

Low Shrub Mass

Evergreens

HOUSE

DRIVEWAY

GARAGE

Walk

Entry

Vines

Walk

Low Shrub Mass

Low Shrub Mass

Large Trees

Lawn

Low Shrub Mass

Vines

Shrub Screen Mass

Close Neighbors

Brick Pillars With Light

OVERCOMING PROBLEMS

Close Driveway—This is a very common architectural problem. On paper it may work, but in the "real world" it tends to create discomfort for the user. A neighbor's driveway that is too close does invade personal space. The design of the property can appear imbalanced as well.

Tall narrow shrubs, massed together, will screen the driveways and give a stronger appearance to the corners of both properties. Many shrubs have this type of growth habit. Most of these can be sheared. This gives you the opportunity to create the shape and height of your choice.

Shrubs and shade trees in the back are arranged to give depth between these two properties. Even as you enter your driveway, the view is oriented diagonally across the yard, drawing your attention away from close neighbors.

67

OVERCOMING PROBLEMS

Cacophony—Believe it or not, noise can be screened efficiently. The more you layer masses of plants together, the more noise control possible. Up to 85% of truck noise and 75% of automobile noise can be reduced.

Evergreen shrubs and trees, deciduous shrubs and trees, and ground covers will all work, but only to a point. You must have a plan. Use evergreen trees with compatible habits, cluster flowering trees of comparable size and shape, and for hedge rows and ground cover, match plant varieties exactly.

One advantage in having to screen noise is that you are encouraged to create your own personal arboretum.

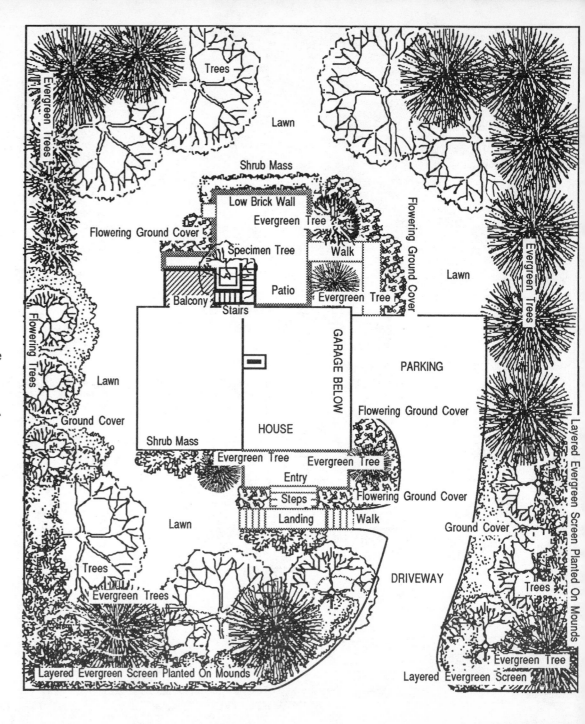

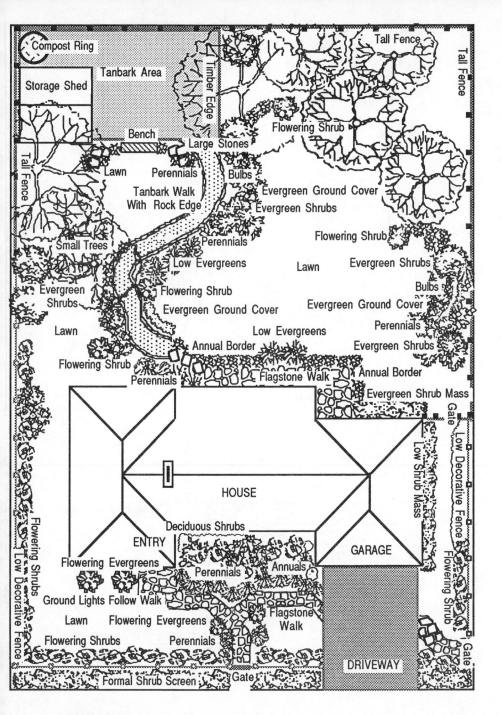

Compost Ring
Storage Shed
Tanbark Area
Timber Edge
Bench
Large Stones
Lawn
Perennials
Bulbs
Tanbark Walk
With Rock Edge
Evergreen Ground Cover
Evergreen Shrubs
Small Trees
Perennials
Flowering Shrub
Low Evergreens
Lawn
Evergreen Shrubs
Evergreen
Shrubs
Flowering Shrub
Evergreen Ground Cover
Bulbs
Evergreen Ground Cover
Perennials
Lawn
Low Evergreens
Annual Border
Evergreen Shrubs
Flowering Shrub
Perennials
Flagstone Walk
Annual Border
Evergreen Shrub Mass
HOUSE
Deciduous Shrubs
ENTRY
GARAGE
Low Shrub Mass
Flowering Evergreens
Annuals
Perennials
Ground Lights
Follow Walk
Flagstone Walk
Lawn
Flowering Evergreens
Perennials
Flowering Shrubs
Low Decorative Fence
Flowering Shrubs
Formal Shrub Screen
Gate
DRIVEWAY
Gate
Low Decorative Fence
Flowering Shrub
Gate
Tall Fence
Tall Fence
Tall Fence
Flowering Shrub

OVERCOMING PROBLEMS

A Necessary Evil—Fence will screen unpleasant views and take up very little room in the landscape, but it should blend with the surroundings. Generally, the less visible a fence the better.

In front, a low fence is screened with hedge for privacy. The inside of the fence is lined with flowering shrubs to break up its sharp angle.

Trees have been used to soften angle of tall fence row along the rear of the property. The effect is somewhat more informal and in keeping with the natural curves of the rear garden. Trees in a variety of sizes will screen the view and allow room for work space and room to garden.

69

OVERCOMING PROBLEMS

Walled In—Change the view and feeling of your garden with a tall masonry wall. The strong screen allows freedom of design. Small lawn, sitting area and large expanse of exposed aggregate paving fit into front yard because of strong separation from outside.

Wall needn't surround entire property. It has been used here where the strongest screening was needed. Shrubbery is planted in rear yard to block unpleasant views.

Notice the absence of foundation plants. At one time they were a necessity to cover unfinished foundations of homes. Today they're unnecessary because most houses are covered to the ground with siding, paneling or other finishing material.

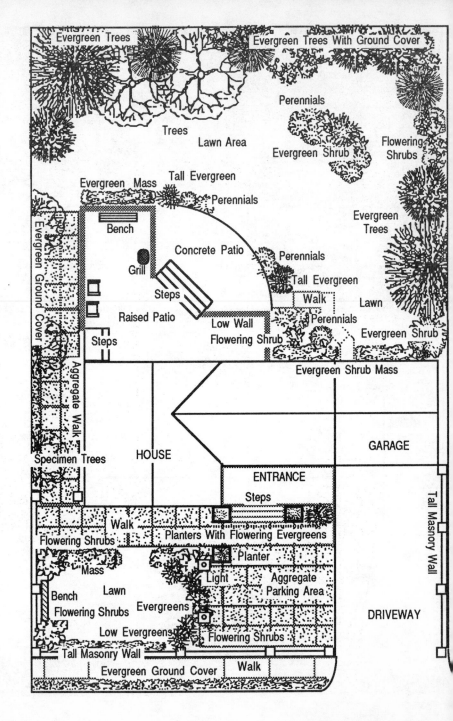

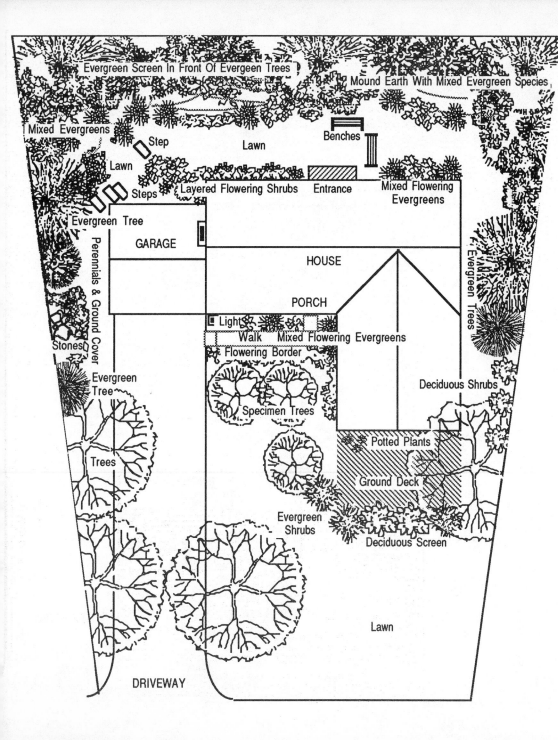

Evergreen Screen In Front Of Evergreen Trees
Mound Earth With Mixed Evergreen Species
Mixed Evergreens
Step
Lawn
Benches
Lawn
Steps
Layered Flowering Shrubs
Entrance
Mixed Flowering Evergreens
Evergreen Tree
GARAGE
HOUSE
Perennials & Ground Cover
Evergreen Trees
PORCH
Light
Walk   Mixed Flowering Evergreens
Flowering Border
Stones
Evergreen Tree
Deciduous Shrubs
Specimen Trees
Trees
Potted Plants
Ground Deck
Evergreen Shrubs
Deciduous Screen
Lawn
DRIVEWAY

OVERCOMING PROBLEMS

U-Shaped Garden—This back yard could be located by a playground, in eyeshot of an industrial park, with northwestern exposure, and the U-shaped barrier planting would screen noise, disguise unpleasant views and block winds.

Plantings around back yard offer a view that one might think leads into woods or wilderness. Benches are set against mounds of soil that are not only instrumental in blocking winds, but strengthen the sense of enclosure as well.

This design makes the most of a shallow back yard. If front of house is situated in a quiet setting, a deck could add depth to the front and provide a sitting and entertaining area as well.

OVERCOMING PROBLEMS

Trapezoid—Except where you're being watched, such as from a nearby neighbor's house, take away the boundaries and design toward a vista. It's a great way to open up cramped spaces.

For total property usage, define space wherever you can find it—such as this side deck, designed for privacy and relaxation.

Screening from the street is achieved by staggering rows of shrubs. This maintains an openness that sets off the front of the house. Entrance courtyard provides an aesthetically pleasing touch for all who enter.

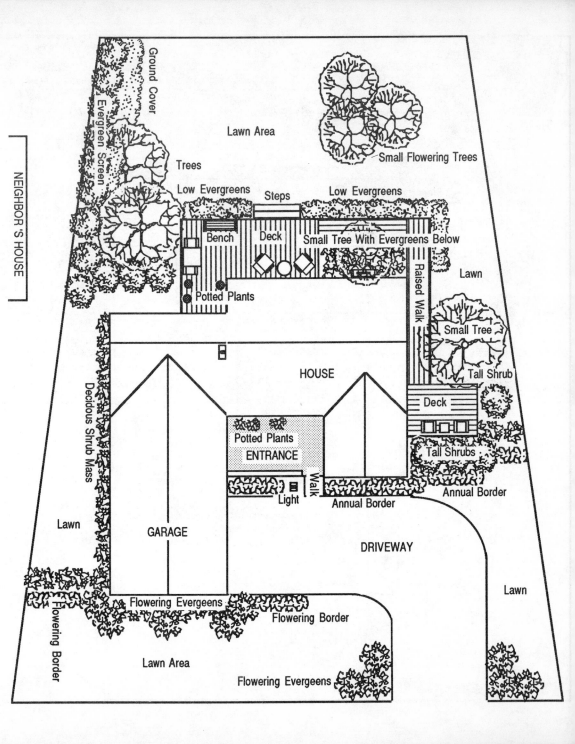

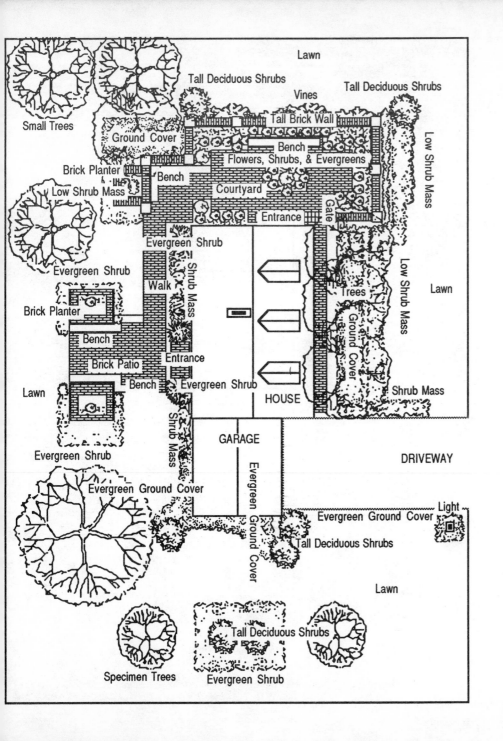

Small Trees

Tall Deciduous Shrubs

Vines

Tall Deciduous Shrubs

Ground Cover

Tall Brick Wall

Low Shrub Mass

Bench

Brick Planter

Flowers, Shrubs, & Evergreens

Bench

Courtyard

Low Shrub Mass

Entrance

Gate

Evergreen Shrub

Evergreen Shrub

Walk

Shrub Mass

Trees

Low Shrub Mass

Lawn

Brick Planter

Ground Cover

Bench

Brick Patio

Entrance

Lawn

Bench

Evergreen Shrub

Shrub Mass

HOUSE

Shrub Mass

Evergreen Shrub

GARAGE

DRIVEWAY

Evergreen Ground Cover

Evergreen Ground Cover

Light

Evergreen Ground Cover

Tall Deciduous Shrubs

Lawn

Specimen Trees

Tall Deciduous Shrubs

Evergreen Shrub

OVERCOMING PROBLEMS

Bricked in Privacy—This design offers an excellent example of what can be achieved through planning. By foreseeing the need to block a view, the plants and structures can be designed accordingly. Here a high degree of privacy has been attained with a tall brick wall.

The brick patio is more comfortable with screening from the neighbors, but not at the expense of the view. Flowers and shrubs surround you, bringing the view close enough to touch.

For a quiet out-of-the-way spot to read or have conversation, use the small deck around back. Brick walk allows for ease of circulation between these two areas, and the view from this deck remains open.

OVERCOMING PROBLEMS

Property Line Design—Trees and shrubs are an excellent hedge against a host of problems. They also serve to define your space. Property line design is a practical and aesthetic use of plant materials, but there's no need to plant them around the entire property. A large planted deck, which has lots of room for outdoor living, offers balance to the tree and shrub masses.

Another way to set off house and lot to their fullest advantage is by entry design. Many interesting effects can be achieved by playing around with lines of entry and paving materials. Here, the driveway winds past ornamental beds and wood walk, mimicking driveway line. Together they present an inviting picture for all who enter.

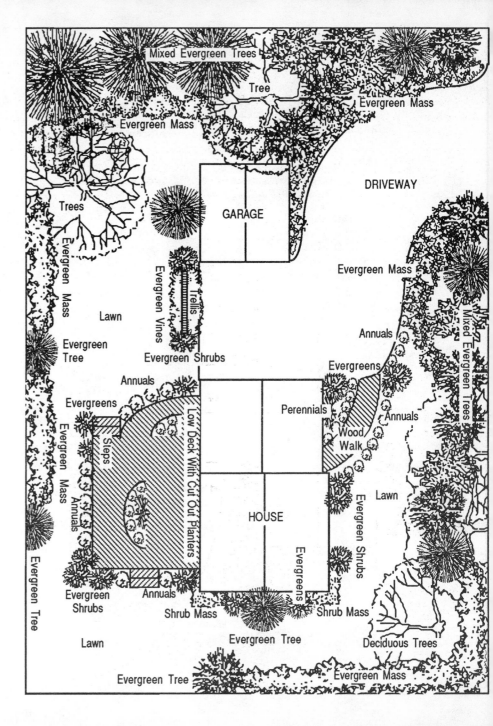

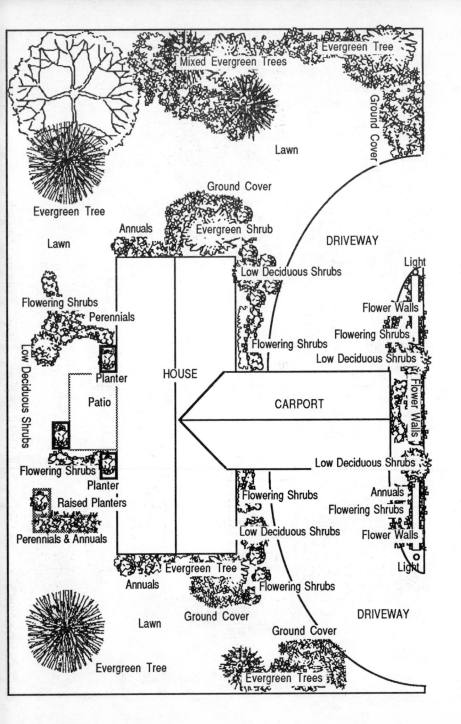

Evergreen Tree
Mixed Evergreen Trees
Ground Cover
Lawn
Evergreen Tree
Lawn
Ground Cover
Annuals
Evergreen Shrub
DRIVEWAY
Light
Low Deciduous Shrubs
Flower Walls
Flowering Shrubs
Perennials
Flowering Shrubs
Low Deciduous Shrubs
Low Deciduous Shrubs
Planter
HOUSE
Patio
CARPORT
Flower Walls
Flowering Shrubs
Planter
Low Deciduous Shrubs
Raised Planters
Annuals
Perennials & Annuals
Flowering Shrubs
Evergreen Tree
Flowering Shrubs
Low Deciduous Shrubs
Flower Walls
Annuals
Lawn
Ground Cover
Light
Evergreen Tree
Ground Cover
DRIVEWAY
Evergreen Trees

OVERCOMING PROBLEMS

Flower Walls---Want to screen traffic or unsightly views? Try flower walls. When a limitation of space cuts your possibilities for screening, why not plant a wall of flowers? It can be constructed with shelves, planters and/or hooks.

Flowers and vines planted along front, placed on top, or on shelves built into wall introduces color and foliage in a unique fashion.

This arrangement would be easy to maintain and keep an eye on because it's so close to the house, and it will be a focal point for all who pass.

PLEASANT VIEWS

Unobstructed—If your property is situated with a vista as far as the eye can see, then you'll want to emphasize that characteristic. An expanse of lawn would allow an unobstructed view.

Plantings have been designed close to the house to soften it and integrate it into the landscape. Relationship of house to landscape is further integrated by patio/planter arrangement, giving a smooth transition from house to lawn.

All paving, plantings and windows should be oriented so that you receive the maximum benefit from your design. This is something that is most effectively done during the preconstruction phase of your project.

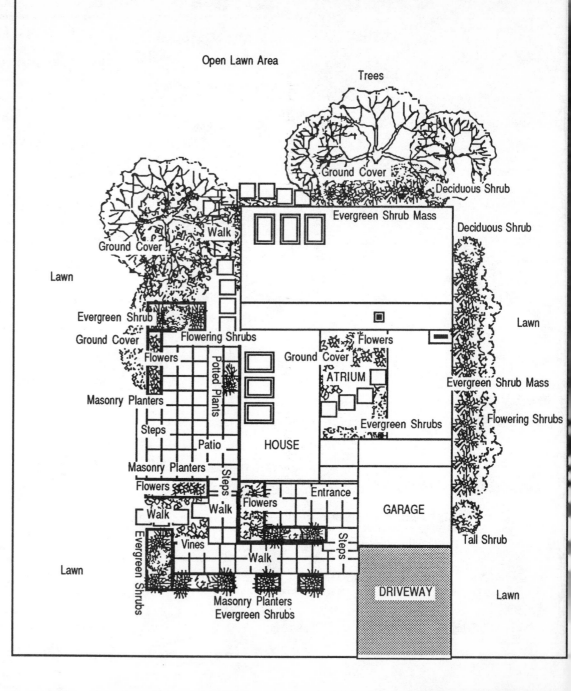

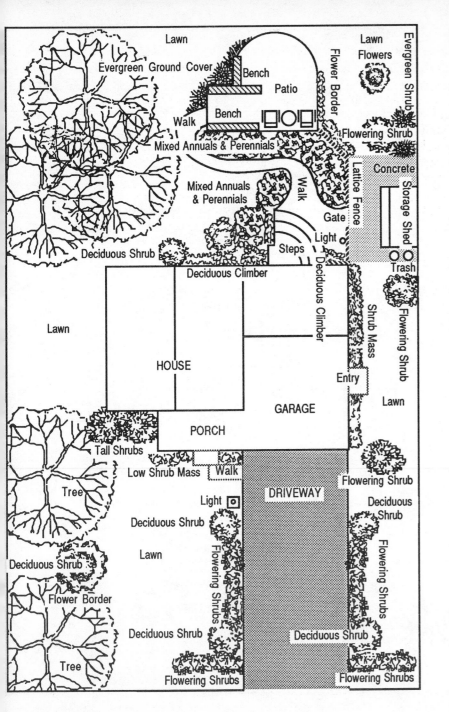

PLEASANT VIEWS

Inviting Vistas—Curved walk leads out the back to view the scenic landscape. Perhaps you border a golf course, look out over a body of water, have a view of mountains and valleys, or simply face the woods. This design takes the patio where the action is. Could you imagine the vantage point for bird watching?

The space between the patio and the house works nicely for a garden area, and the stroll through the garden is as enjoyable as your view out the back.

A lattice fence screens the storage shed to maintain a pleasing view in the garden area. Curved steps match the curve of the patio to further enhance this garden.

PLEASANT VIEWS

Natural Backdrop—The rear of this property has an open orientation, and the trellis-covered picnic area and central ornamental planting uses what lies beyond as a backdrop. Almost any view would do: neighbor's landscaping, common land in the development, or any arrangement of plants in the landscape.

With this shallow front yard, you'll be in luck if you have plantings adjacent to your property that fit your home and tastes. Should you have such a pleasant setting, a wide entrance with matching specimen trees will offer appealing spaciousness to your home.

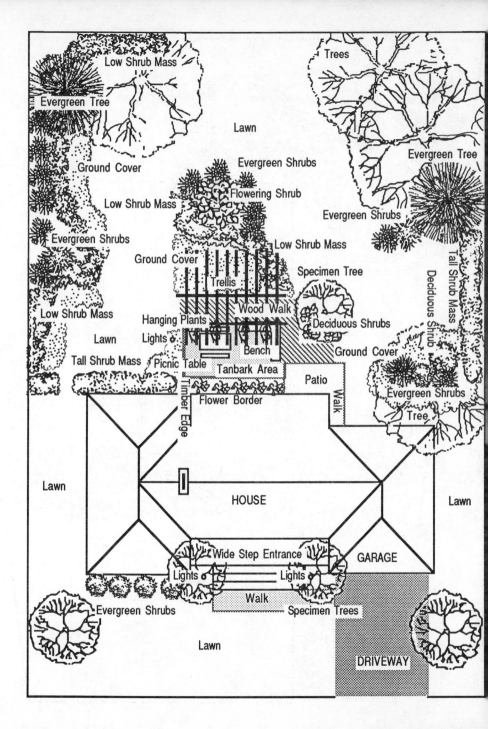

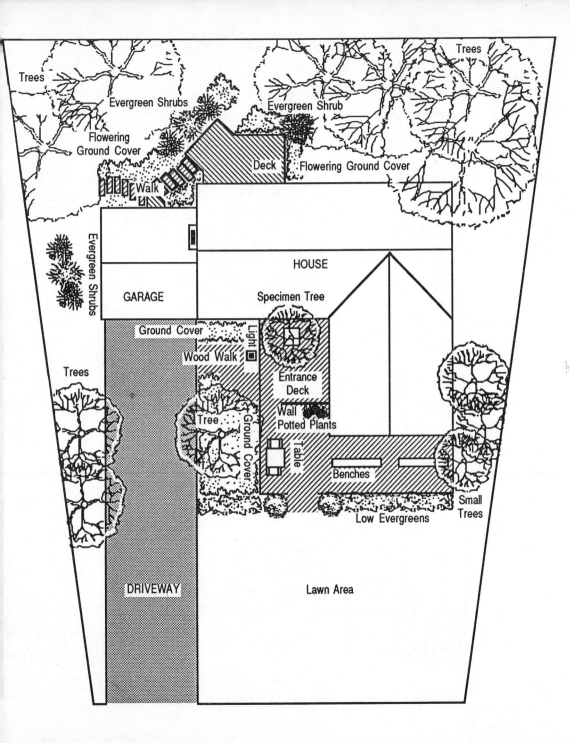

Trees

Evergreen Shrubs

Flowering Ground Cover

Evergreen Shrub

Deck Flowering Ground Cover

Trees

Walk

Evergreen Shrubs

HOUSE

GARAGE

Specimen Tree

Ground Cover

Light

Wood Walk

Trees

Tree

Entrance Deck

Ground Cover

Wall Potted Plants

Table

Benches

Low Evergreens

Small Trees

DRIVEWAY

Lawn Area

PLEASANT VIEWS

Multi-Use Deck—One of the basic considerations for adding interest to a property is to identify pleasant views and incorporate them into the design. Here, the pleasant view is toward the front of the house. Therefore, the front deck has been specially designed to include entrance and separate recreational space.

Stepped entrance walk brings visitors around lighting, under tree and up to the front door. A wooden wall and small specimen tree clearly define this area. Around the wall is a separate patio with table, seating and container plants.

If you plant a canopy of large trees in the rear yard, they won't block your view and they'll create a massing effect over the roof level of the house, tying the house to the landscape.

PLEASANT VIEWS

Garden Collection—Some of the finest gardens in the world are merely composites of many smaller gardens. This property has been made into three smaller garden areas—entrance garden, garden court and vista garden. Each area has a specific use and personality.

Entrance garden aesthetically enhances the front and invites visitor into the house. Three large and three small trees offer a screening effect from the street.

The planting court provides circulation from the house to the rear garden. Curved walk and enclosure from the wings of the house make this space into a separate garden area.

The vista garden has paths and plant arrangements giving the garden interest in and of itself, and has a vista giving it interest outside of itself as well.

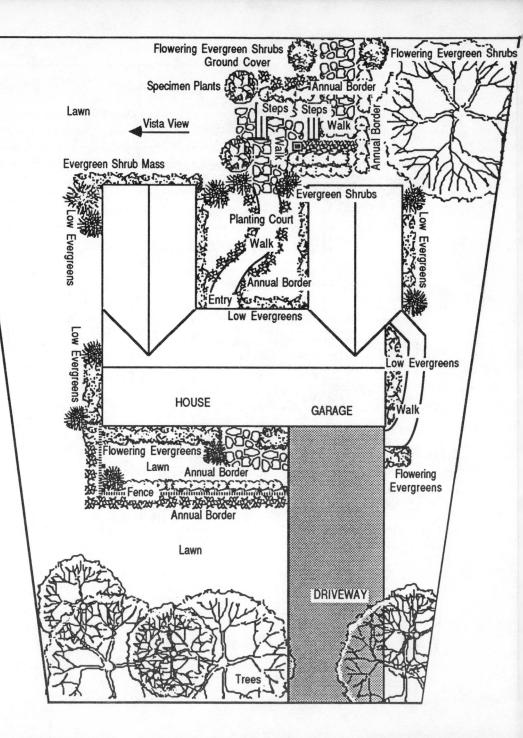

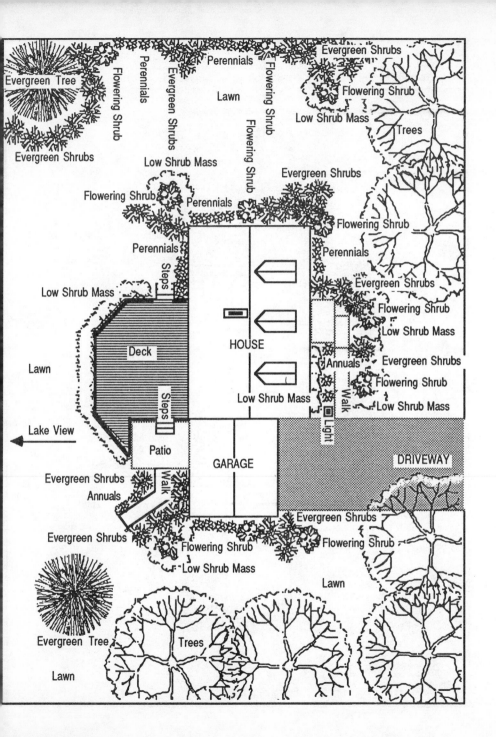

Evergreen Tree

Perennials

Flowering Shrub

Evergreen Shrubs

Perennials

Evergreen Shrubs

Lawn

Perennials

Evergreen Shrubs

Flowering Shrub

Flowering Shrub

Flowering Shrub

Low Shrub Mass

Trees

Low Shrub Mass

Flowering Shrub

Perennials

Evergreen Shrubs

Flowering Shrub

Perennials

Perennials

Flowering Shrub

Low Shrub Mass

Steps

Evergreen Shrubs

Flowering Shrub

Perennials

HOUSE

Deck

Low Shrub Mass

Evergreen Shrubs

Lawn

Steps

Annuals

Flowering Shrub

Walk

Evergreen Shrubs

Lake View

Low Shrub Mass

Low Shrub Mass

Light

Patio

Steps

Walk

GARAGE

DRIVEWAY

Evergreen Shrubs

Annuals

Evergreen Shrubs

Evergreen Shrubs

Flowering Shrub

Flowering Shrub

Low Shrub Mass

Lawn

Evergreen Tree

Trees

Lawn

PLEASANT VIEWS

Lake View—House and garden are designed to get the most from a view of the lake. Heavily treed and planted front garden partially hide lake from street and provide private enclosure for residents. Deck overlooks the water.

If you live at the water's edge, deck design can be repeated in the form of a dock. This could serve as a fishing, sunning, reading, boating, swimming and entertaining area, depending upon your local regulations.

PLEASANT VIEWS

Curved in Stone—Circular patio and stone paving tie this design together. The patio also introduces curvilinear form to a strongly rectilinear house and property. This integrates the house with the land.

Another integrative feature of all landscape design is plant material. Since most angles in nature are not 90°, plants soften the harsh lines of the built environment and bring it into balance with nature.

The plantings and patio also serve to orient the user toward the view. Although the house does not have windows facing the scenic area, many outdoor areas have been designed to lead your eye in the direction of distant attractions.

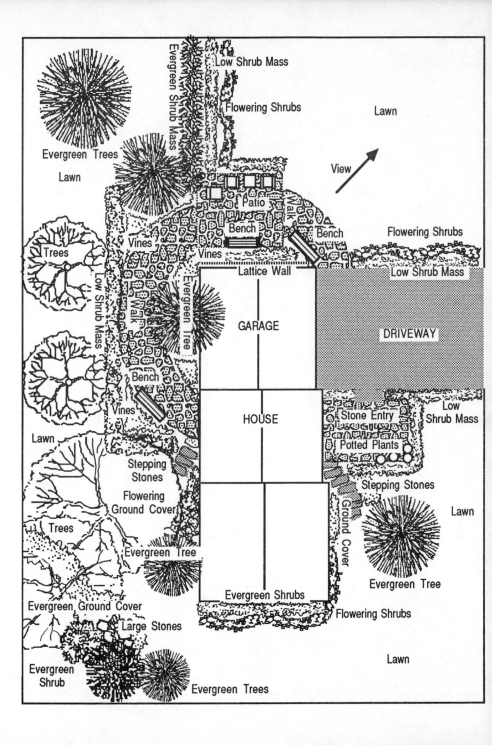

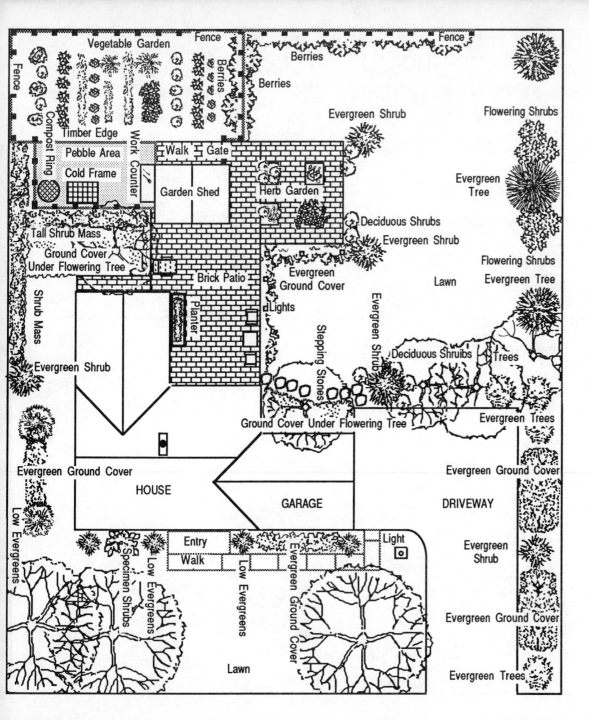

Vegetable Garden

Fence

Berries

Berries

Berries

Fence

Compost Ring

Timber Edge

Pebble Area

Cold Frame

Work Counter

Walk

Gate

Garden Shed

Herb Garden

Evergreen Shrub

Flowering Shrubs

Evergreen Tree

Fence

Tall Shrub Mass

Ground Cover Under Flowering Tree

Shrub Mass

Evergreen Shrub

Brick Patio

Planter

Lights

Evergreen Ground Cover

Deciduous Shrubs

Evergreen Shrub

Flowering Shrubs

Evergreen Tree

Lawn

Stepping Stones

Evergreen Shrub

Deciduous Shrubs

Trees

Ground Cover Under Flowering Tree

Evergreen Trees

Evergreen Ground Cover

Evergreen Ground Cover

Low Evergreens

Specimen Shrubs

Low Evergreens

Low Evergreens

Evergreen Ground Cover

Entry

Walk

Light

Evergreen Shrub

HOUSE

GARAGE

DRIVEWAY

Lawn

Evergreen Ground Cover

Evergreen Trees

SPECIALTY GARDENS

Aesthetic Edibles—Planning gives you the opportunity to consider every angle before installation. The angles here include vegetables, herbs, berries, work and storage area without sacrificing aesthetics.

The brick patio, with spaces for planting, makes the perfect herb garden and sitting area. Small spaces contain the herbs and keep them manicured in appearance. The vegetable garden and work areas are also incorporated into the brick patio. They are separated from the viewer by a fence and shed combination, which serves to screen garden from view as well as from rabbits, gophers and chipmunks.

An extra section of fence across the back can screen the property and serve as a support and backdrop for your berry patch.

SPECIALTY GARDENS

Progressive Realization—This informal landscape is filled with private gardens, sitting areas and sculpture. Shrubs and flowers are arranged to hide one part of the garden from another. In this way you cannot see the entire property from a single vantage point. The interest this introduces to your property is mystery—the mystery of what lies beyond, and it's something that has always drawn people into the landscape.

Sculpture offers even more excitement when discovered among the shrubbery. Seating has been placed at points of interest along the paths to encourage hesitation at the various focal points.

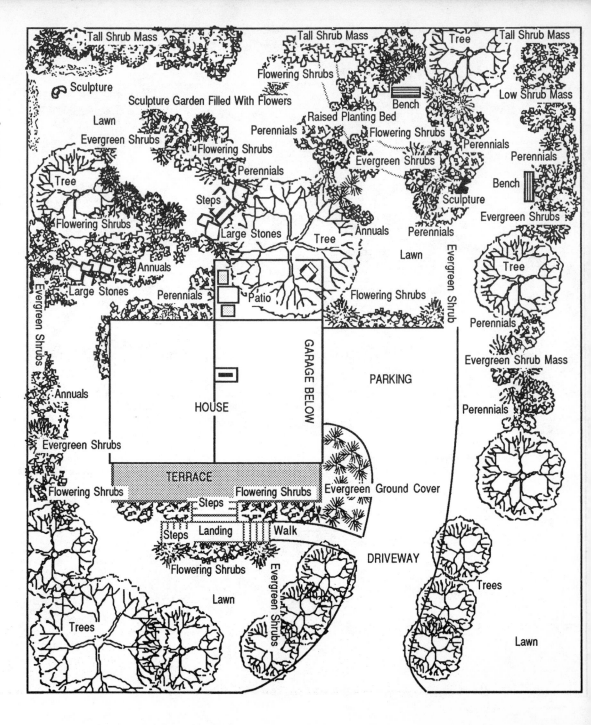

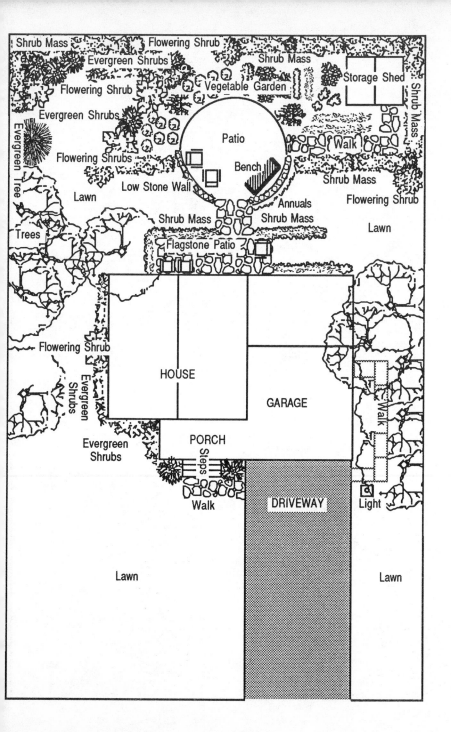

Shrub Mass · Flowering Shrub
Evergreen Shrubs · Shrub Mass
Flowering Shrub · Vegetable Garden · Storage Shed
Evergreen Shrubs
Patio · Walk
Flowering Shrubs · Bench
Lawn · Low Stone Wall · Shrub Mass
Trees · Annuals · Flowering Shrub
Shrub Mass · Shrub Mass · Lawn
Flowering Shrub · Flagstone Patio
HOUSE · GARAGE
Flowering Shrub · Evergreen Shrubs
Evergreen Shrubs · PORCH · Walk
Steps · Light
Walk · DRIVEWAY
Lawn · Lawn

SPECIALTY GARDENS

Vegetables Incorporated—The round patio doubles as a platform for working in the vegetable garden. Stone walk to storage shed also offers access to vegetables. If you design vegetables with ornamental considerations, you will have incorporated the practical with the beautiful.

This garden exemplifies the basic philosophy of landscape design—manipulate the environment to create function and beauty.

The rest of the property is designed with an open expanse of lawn to the front and massed deciduous tress along both sides. This widens the look of the property, giving a spacious appearance to the front of the house.

SPECIALTY GARDENS

Raised Vegetables—Level changes give interest to a property, especially a flat one. Sunken patio and raised planters create places to plant vegetables ornamentally, where during times of peak growth, they serve as strong enclosure for the patio. Raised planters make weeding and harvest enjoyable and easy as well.

In front, concrete retaining wall offers level change along driveway, and visitors walk down two steps onto the entry patio. Raised planters and nicely sequenced plants against the house carry this sunken garden effect into the front yard.

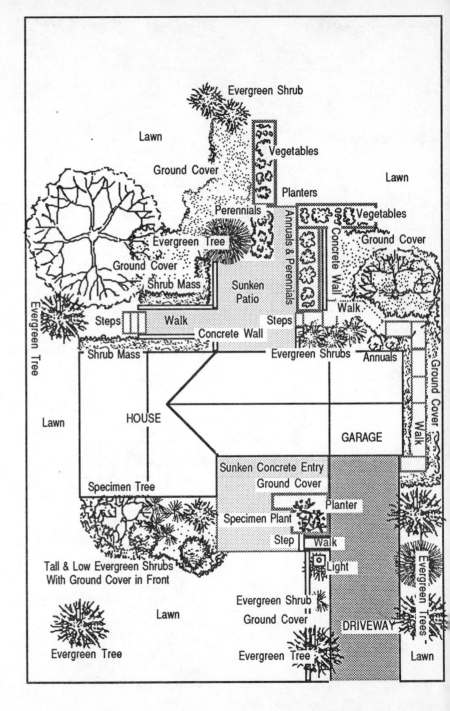

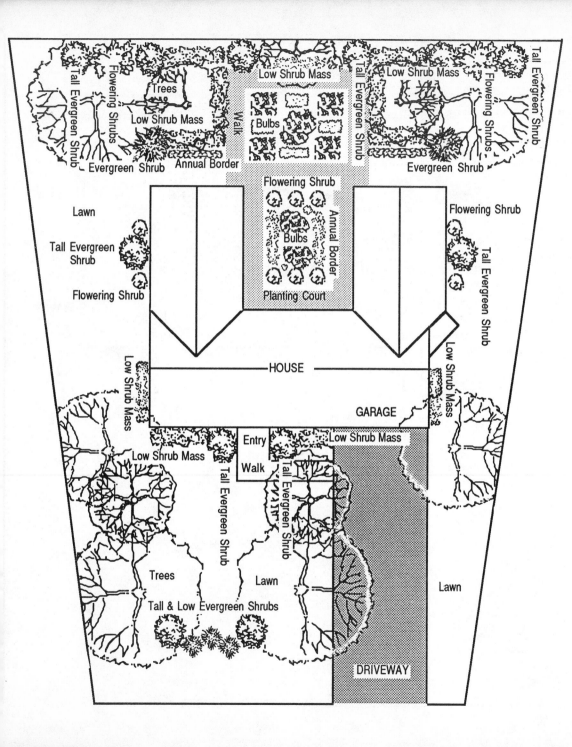

Tall Evergreen Shrub
Flowering Shrubs
Trees
Low Shrub Mass
Low Shrub Mass
Walk
Low Shrub Mass
Low Shrub Mass
Tall Evergreen Shrub
Flowering Shrubs
Tall Evergreen Shrub
Evergreen Shrub
Annual Border
Bulbs
Evergreen Shrub

Lawn
Tall Evergreen Shrub
Flowering Shrub
Flowering Shrub
Annual Border
Flowering Shrub
Bulbs
Planting Court
Tall Evergreen Shrub

HOUSE
Low Shrub Mass
GARAGE
Low Shrub Mass

Low Shrub Mass
Entry
Walk
Low Shrub Mass
Low Shrub Mass

Tall Evergreen Shrub
Tall Evergreen Shrub
Trees
Lawn
Lawn
Tall & Low Evergreen Shrubs
DRIVEWAY

SPECIALTY GARDENS

Formal Symmetry—Symmetry tends to imply formality in design. This somewhat informal front entry gives way to the extremely formal rear garden as a focal point. The colors are part of the reason for focus in the back yard, but the main aspect of interest is the strong sense of symmetrical balance. Equal plantings of flowers, shrubs and trees have been used. Even the sides of the house have exactly the same arrangements as one another.

The front of the house is difficult to design symmetrically because most homes today have garage or entry to one side. A rounded driveway can help to present a more formal appearance.

SPECIALTY GARDENS

An Oriental Flavor—You can achieve an oriental feel to the garden with simplicity—few plant varieties; simple, flowing lines; and basic construction materials.

Develop ways to mimic nature. Create a pebbled sea. Sit by the shore under shade trellis. Include a favorite sculptural piece to contemplate on the opposite shore.

Flowers are used in a natural setting, and bamboo type foliage lends an oriental flavor.

Note: Use only dwarf bamboos or Nandina, since full size bamboo is too prolific and in many climates will take over garden.

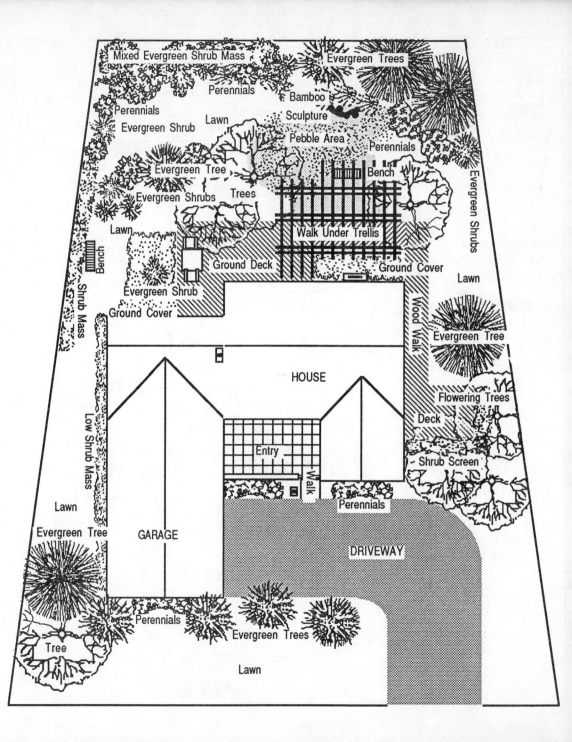

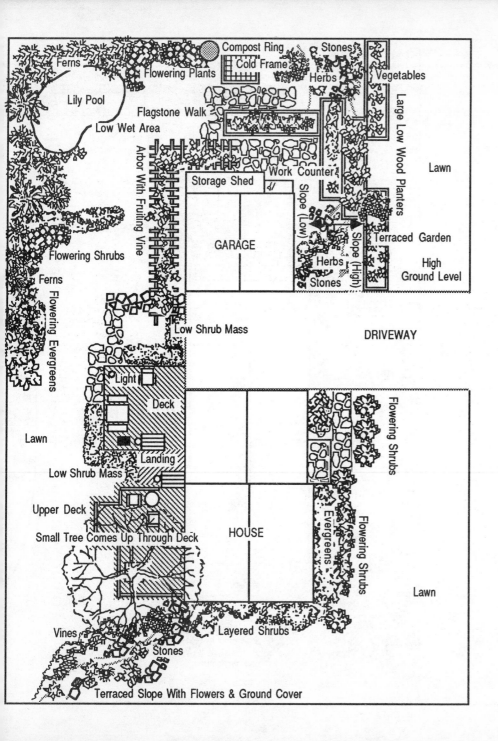

Ferns
Flowering Plants
Compost Ring
Cold Frame
Stones
Herbs
Vegetables
Lily Pool
Flagstone Walk
Low Wet Area
Arbor With Fruiting Vine
Work Counter
Storage Shed
Slope (Low)
Slope (Low)
Large Low Wood Planters
Lawn
GARAGE
Slope (High)
Terraced Garden
High Ground Level
Herbs
Stones
Flowering Shrubs
Ferns
Flowering Evergreens
Low Shrub Mass
DRIVEWAY
Light
Deck
Flowering Shrubs
Lawn
Landing
Low Shrub Mass
Upper Deck
Small Tree Comes Up Through Deck
HOUSE
Flowering Evergreens
Flowering Shrubs
Lawn
Vines
Stones
Layered Shrubs
Terraced Slope With Flowers & Ground Cover

SPECIALTY GARDENS

Harmonious Hills—Sloping yards are adaptable to many sorts of features. Lily pool, terraced wooden planters, herb/rock garden and arbor walk are all harmonious with the design of hilly properties.

The lily pool should fit the contours of the land to look like it belongs, and water should drain away from edges of pool.

Stepped wood planters and herb/rock garden fit the front contour leading up to the house. Planters will create level planting areas on the slope.

SPECIALTY GARDENS

Diagonal Deck—Why not a diagonal deck when back yard is too shallow for an expansive outdoor living area? The deck has room for planters, table and chairs, and sitting and sunning areas. Entry from the formal driveway is easy. There are a variety of views, and both the front and back of the property can be enjoyed from the deck.

On deck side of house, shrubs and bedding plants fit deck into landscaping and maintain sunny orientation. The property is balanced to the opposite side with a number of shade trees and shrub masses.

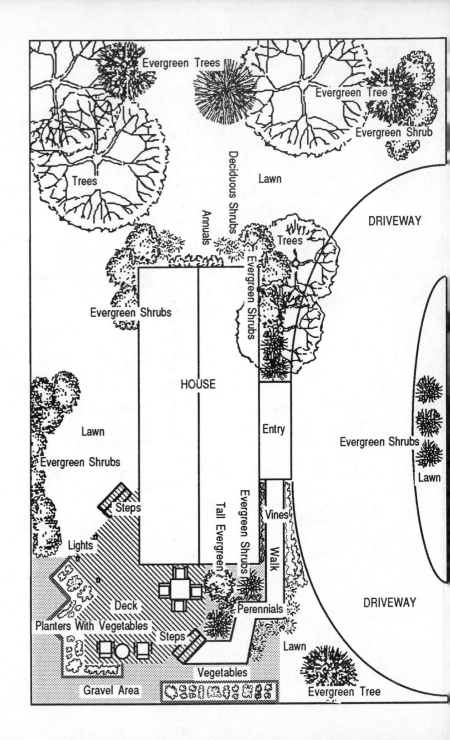

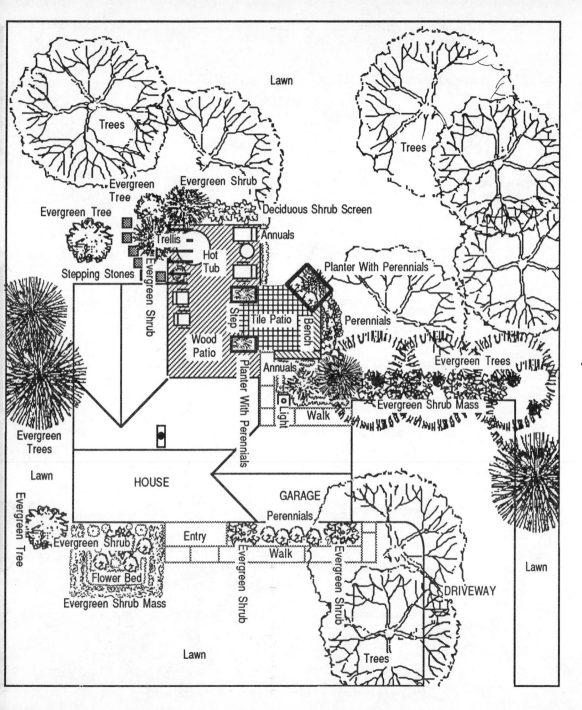

Lawn

Trees

Evergreen Tree

Evergreen Shrub

Evergreen Tree

Trees

Deciduous Shrub Screen

Trellis

Annuals

Hot Tub

Planter With Perennials

Stepping Stones

Evergreen Shrub

Step

Tile Patio

Bench

Perennials

Wood Patio

Annuals

Evergreen Trees

Planter With Perennials

Light

Walk

Evergreen Shrub Mass

Evergreen Trees

Lawn

Evergreen Tree

HOUSE

GARAGE

Perennials

Evergreen Tree

Evergreen Shrub

Entry

Walk

Evergreen Shrub

Evergreen Shrub

Lawn

Flower Bed

DRIVEWAY

Evergreen Shrub Mass

Trees

Lawn

FOUNTAINS/POOLS/HOT TUBS

Bathing Beauty—You'll want a sunny orientation for the hot tub, but it's the type of water feature that's best in a private setting. In this design, hot tub is screened with shade trellis, shrub screen and an evergreen shrub mass at the end of driveway. The house furnishes enclosure as well.

In many locales, hot tubs are usable 11-12 months of the year. Even during the colder periods the hot tub will still maintain a comfortable temperature.

Plant your patio with flowers and hang baskets on trellis by hot tub. Bilevel patio and deck arrangement makes bathing beautiful.

FOUNTAINS/POOLS/HOT TUBS

Pretty Secure—Swimming pool is surrounded by fence, keeping it secure and meeting city code and insurance requirements in most states. It's not done at the expense of beauty. In fact, it enhances the property in this design.

A pool-garden arrangement softens the impact that a swimming pool usually has on the landscape. Vines covering fence and shade trellis create a comfortable enclosure.

Flowers and shrubs extend the planting areas outside the fence, add dimension to the garden and screen the view of the fence. The security's there and the aesthetics don't suffer.

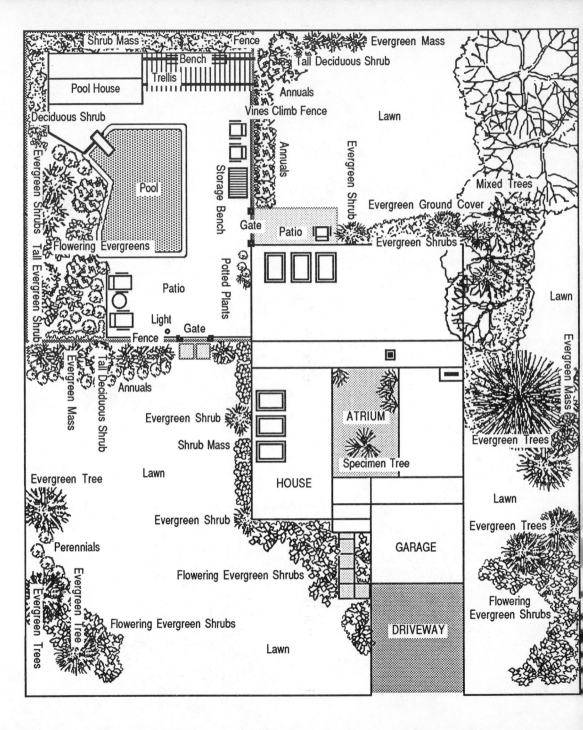

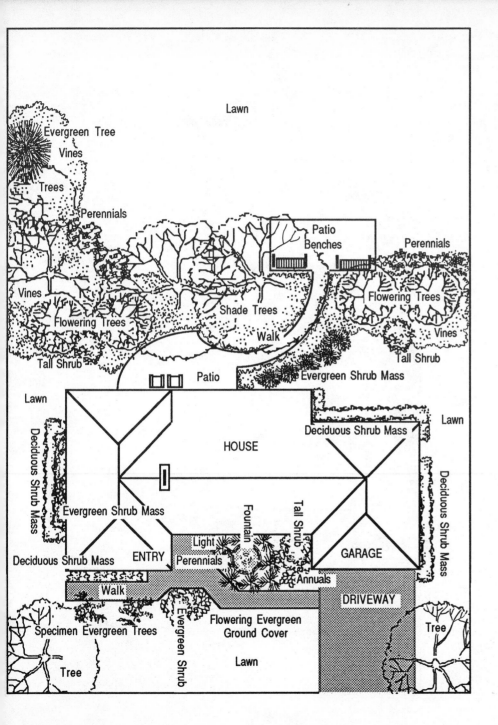

Lawn

Evergreen Tree

Vines

Trees

Perennials

Vines

Flowering Trees

Tall Shrub

Patio
Benches

Perennials

Shade Trees

Walk

Flowering Trees

Vines

Tall Shrub

Lawn

Patio

Evergreen Shrub Mass

Deciduous Shrub Mass

Lawn

Deciduous Shrub Mass

HOUSE

Deciduous Shrub Mass

Evergreen Shrub Mass

Fountain

Tall Shrub

Deciduous Shrub Mass

ENTRY

Light

Perennials

GARAGE

Annuals

Walk

DRIVEWAY

Specimen Evergreen Trees

Evergreen Shrub

Flowering Evergreen
Ground Cover

Lawn

Tree

Tree

FOUNTAINS/POOLS/HOT TUBS

Naturally Formal—Fountain at front window and shrubs massed into front walk grace the entry of this home. As visitors approach, shrubs direct attention toward the fountain. Walk extends along front of house, defining the planting bed. The fountain and balanced walk imply formality in this design.

Before installing fountain, search for one that fits your personality. Many types will work—from handmade metal or ceramic, to commercial precast—or design your own.

The patio that adjoins the back of house is a unique configuration bringing natural flowing lines into natural flowing landscape. The patio situated on the edge of the woods is oriented toward back lawn area.

FOUNTAINS/POOLS/HOT TUBS

Color, Movement and Light—A series of wooden pads lead you through the perennials and evergreens to the lily pool. The pool can be done in concrete or with a plastic liner. Concrete patio around edge can be paved in exposed aggregate to make the texture more harmonious with the environment. Plantings to the back of the pool integrate it into the rear garden.

Standing by the water's edge brings you close to fragrant lilies and colorful aquatic life. Sitting on the deck offers another perspective. Enjoy color, movement and the play of light on the water's surface.

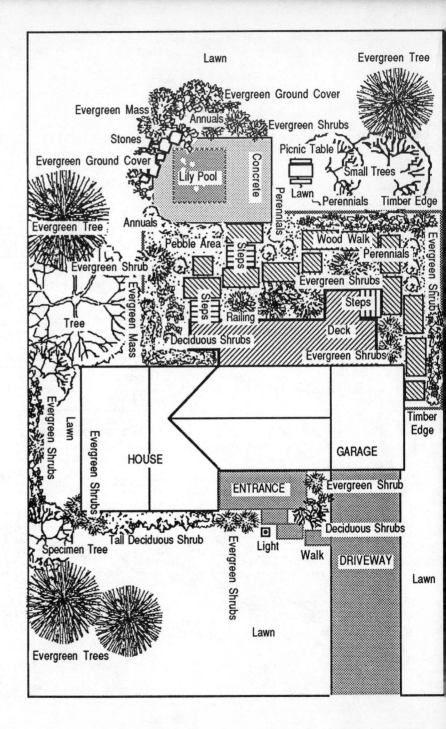

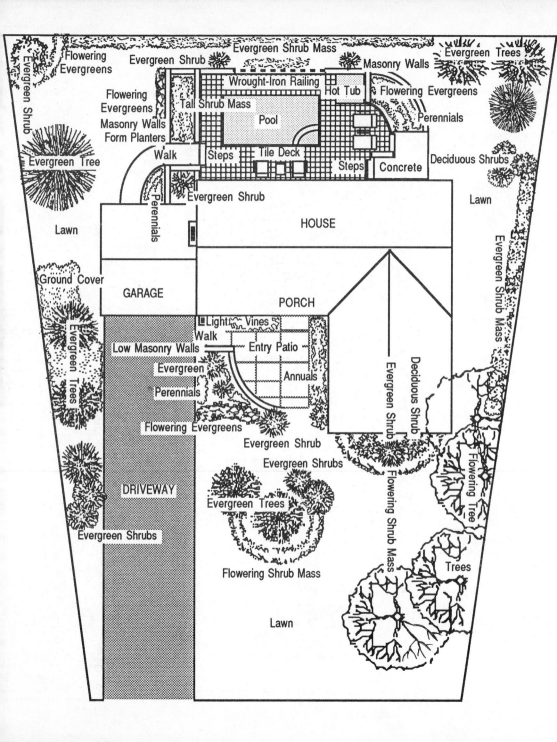

Flowering Evergreens
Evergreen Shrub
Evergreen Shrub Mass
Evergreen Trees
Masonry Walls
Flowering Evergreens
Wrought-Iron Railing
Hot Tub
Tall Shrub Mass
Pool
Perennials
Flowering Evergreens
Masonry Walls Form Planters
Walk
Steps
Tile Deck
Deciduous Shrubs
Steps
Concrete
Evergreen Shrub
Evergreen Tree
Evergreen Shrub
Perennials
Lawn
HOUSE
Lawn
Ground Cover
GARAGE
PORCH
Evergreen Trees
Light
Vines
Walk
Low Masonry Walls
Entry Patio
Evergreen
Perennials
Annuals
Evergreen Shrub Mass
Flowering Evergreens
Evergreen Shrub
Deciduous Shrub
Evergreen Shrubs
Flowering Shrub Mass
Evergreen Trees
Flowering Tree
DRIVEWAY
Evergreen Shrubs
Flowering Shrub Mass
Trees
Lawn

FOUNTAINS/POOLS/HOT TUBS

Somewhat Different—Masonry walls form planters, hot tub and pool deck. Wrought-iron railing connects the walls to complete enclosure of pool. The surface of the deck is done in tile for an unusual ornamental touch.

The masonry wall theme is carried to the front, creating an entrance court.

Privacy is achieved with a variety of plantings. Tall evergreen shrub masses, evergreen trees and small flowering trees are used around the property line for screening.

FOUNTAINS/POOLS/HOT TUBS

Oriental Flair—This design has an oriental flair that will make you feel as though you were in a Japanese bathhouse. All you need are the geisha girls.

Step down into hot tub from raised deck. Stone area surrounding pool creates a low-care surface close to the water, and the deck provides strong enclosure. Mixed plantings, some distance from the deck, offer beauty as well as screening.

Even more privacy is offered around the side of the house on a tightly enclosed deck, covered by shade trellis.

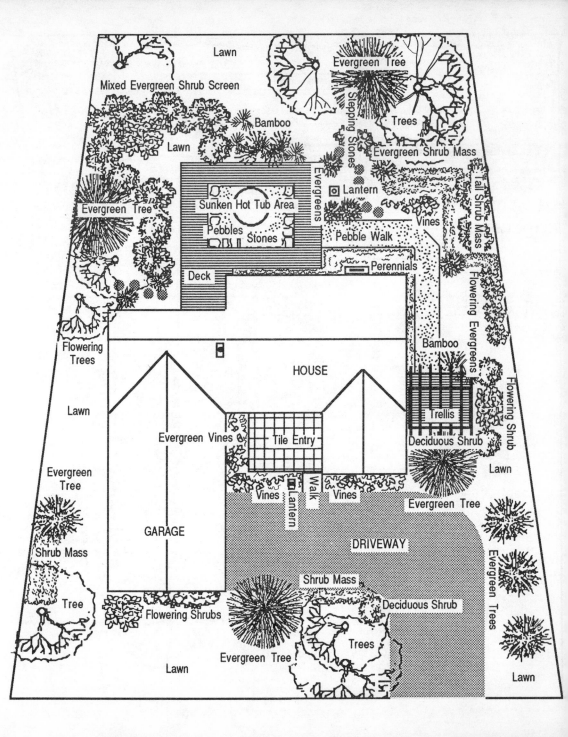

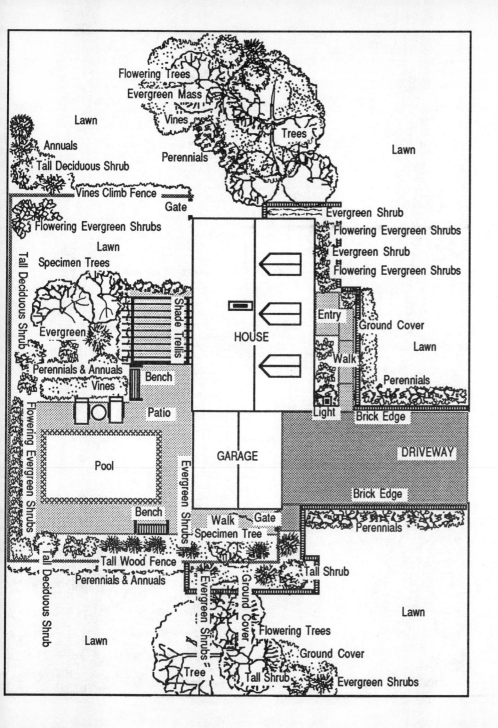

Flowering Trees
Evergreen Mass
Vines
Trees
Lawn
Annuals
Tall Deciduous Shrub
Perennials
Lawn
Vines Climb Fence
Gate
Evergreen Shrub
Flowering Evergreen Shrubs
Flowering Evergreen Shrubs
Evergreen Shrub
Lawn
Flowering Evergreen Shrubs
Specimen Trees
Tall Deciduous Shrub
Shade Trellis
HOUSE
Entry
Ground Cover
Evergreen
Lawn
Walk
Perennials & Annuals
Bench
Vines
Perennials
Patio
Light
Brick Edge
Pool
DRIVEWAY
Flowering Evergreen Shrubs
Evergreen Shrubs
GARAGE
Brick Edge
Bench
Walk
Gate
Perennials
Specimen Tree
Tall Wood Fence
Tall Shrub
Perennials & Annuals
Evergreen Shrubs
Ground Cover
Tall Deciduous Shrub
Lawn
Flowering Trees
Lawn
Ground Cover
Tree
Tall Shrub
Evergreen Shrubs

FOUNTAINS/POOLS/HOT TUBS

Estate-Like—Brick edging and fence outline the use areas. Massed trees, flowers and vines extend house line to the edge of the property. This gives an estate-like characteristic. Swimming pool and shaded sitting area add the finishing touches.

Although total separation between public and private space is created by the fence, it is a rather rigid structure for the landscape. Therefore, the line is broken up with shrubs that partially hide the fence.

Long hedge rows can get boring and start to appear as fences. A variety of plants in different arrangements will give more interest to the design and break up fence row more effectively.

97

FOUNTAINS/POOLS/HOT TUBS

Wraparound Lily Pool—A diagonal line creates living space all the way to the back of this property. Diagonals imply movement in the landscape; therefore, the two patios to the rear flow into one another.

The lily pool can also add movement to the garden by using bubble fountain, lily pads, fish and/or just the rippling effect caused by the wind. Done in a wraparound fashion, the pool surrounds the user, encouraging movement, either visually or physically, around the patio.

Lighting adds another dimension to the garden by offering night interest as well.

Tuck this arrangement into massed shrubbery and flowers for a backdrop that gives stability and comfort to this design.

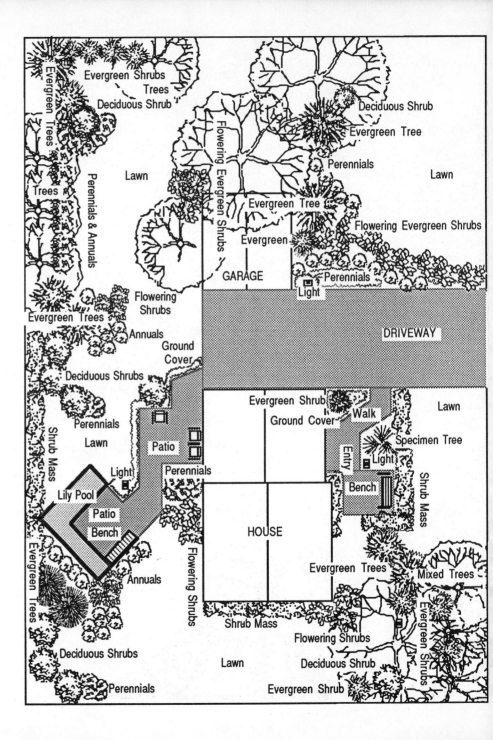

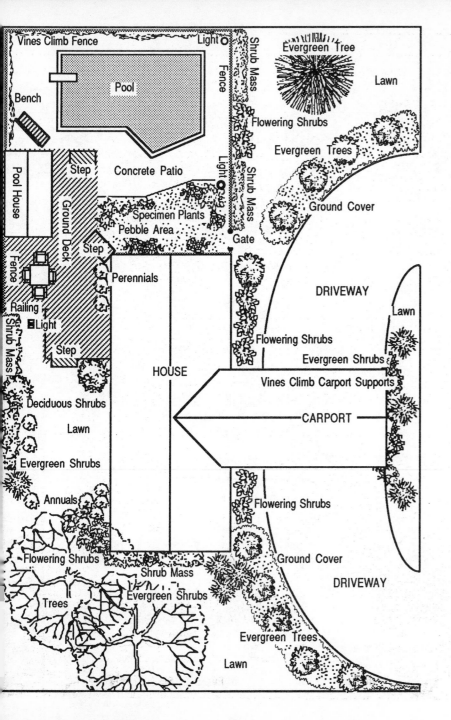

FOUNTAINS/POOLS/HOT TUBS

Efficient Space Usage—This extremely shallow back yard needn't keep you from having every garden feature you desire. The pool is set off to the side of the property and connected to the house with a deck. A vine-covered fence surrounds pool and offers a low-maintenance wall of greenery without using lots of room.

This arrangement has interest for a number of reasons. It introduces a variety of level changes, offers a small specimen garden, visible from both deck and pool, and it exemplifies what can be done with an otherwise flat area.

SPECIALTY STRUCTURES

Gazebo Garden—One of the basic tenets for using a gazebo, springhouse or other garden structure in English design is to have a spot where you can escape to. This design fits this criterion exceptionally well. Masses of shrubbery and trees effectively divide gazebo vista from other views or vantage points on property.

The path makes circulation through the garden easy and offers continuity. From rear patio to gazebo, across stepping stones to drive, or from gazebo to patio at end of driveway, this garden fits the theories of English Natural garden design.

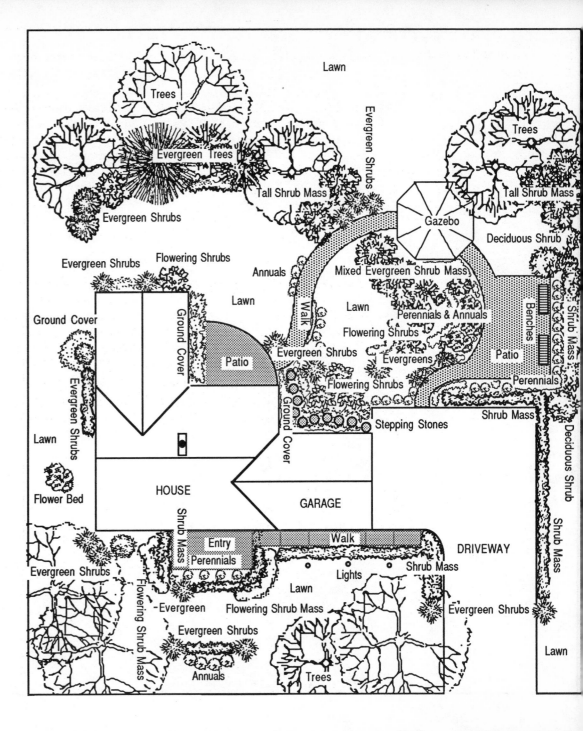

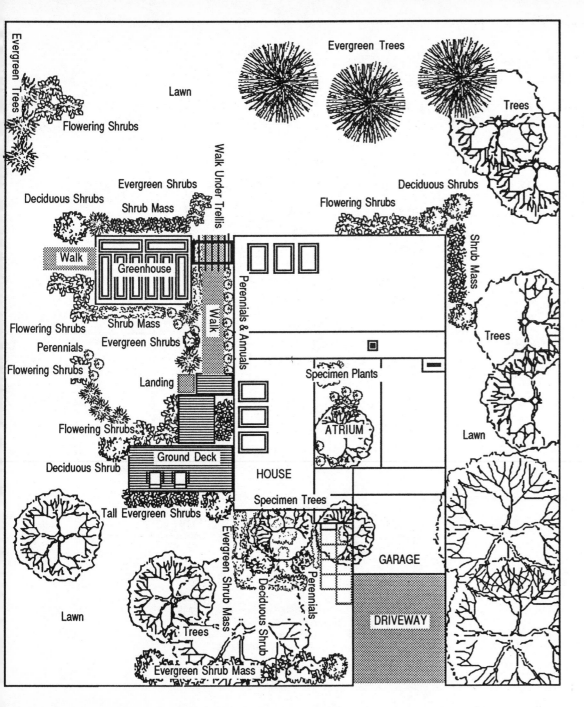

Evergreen Trees

Lawn

Evergreen Trees

Trees

Flowering Shrubs

Evergreen Shrubs

Walk Under Trellis

Deciduous Shrubs

Deciduous Shrubs

Shrub Mass

Flowering Shrubs

Shrub Mass

Walk

Greenhouse

Perennials & Annuals

Shrub Mass

Walk

Flowering Shrubs

Trees

Perennials

Evergreen Shrubs

Flowering Shrubs

Landing

Specimen Plants

Flowering Shrubs

ATRIUM

Lawn

Deciduous Shrub

Ground Deck

HOUSE

Tall Evergreen Shrubs

Specimen Trees

Evergreen Shrub Mass

Deciduous Shrub

Perennials

GARAGE

Lawn

Trees

DRIVEWAY

Evergreen Shrub Mass

SPECIALTY STRUCTURES

Useful and Contemporary—The more avid a gardener you are the more structures you need in the garden, such as potting, storage, seeding and even plant-testing areas. But the ultimate dream for the serious gardener is to have a greenhouse. The beauty of a greenhouse is that you can have these areas and more under one roof. Storage, potting and propagating are easily achieved as long as your structure is planned carefully.

Be sure to include indoor as well as outdoor plants. Grow flowers for cutting or vegetables for planting in the spring.

Solar greenhouses or other contemporary structures would fit in beautifully with this garden. The open skylight and atrium design of the house lends itself well to this landscape design.

SPECIALTY STRUCTURES

Castle Garden—Your home can have the appearance of a mountain cabin or a castle, depending upon the height and style of the stone fence. During the castle garden period, the wall fulfilled the need for security, and gardens and living space were tightly enclosed within tall stone structures.

In this design the wall bends around to enclose the patio and the house. Vine-covered wood fence continues the line of enclosure to the rear, where shrub screen and trees are used.

Be sure to design for 12-month interest and for all your senses in order to make your bastion not only secure, but a pleasure to behold.

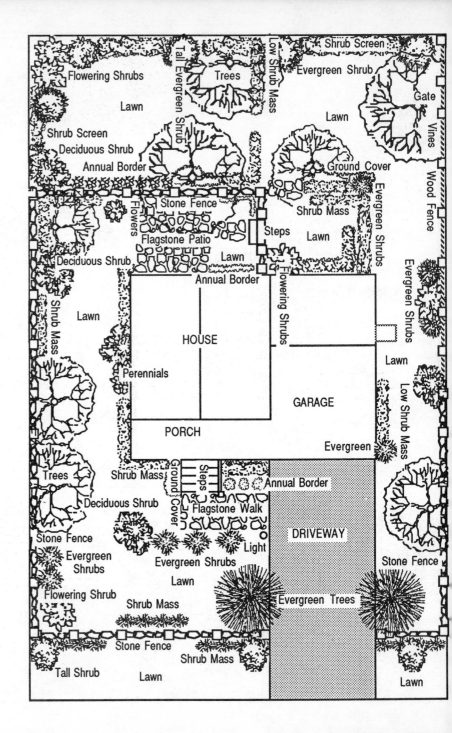

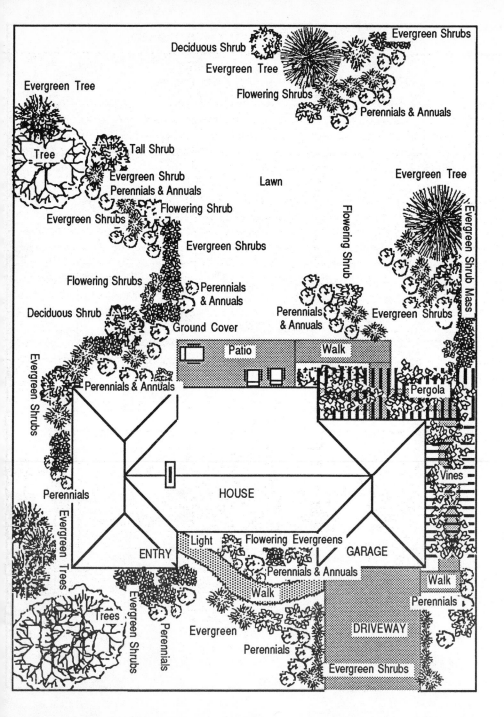

The figure is labeled throughout with: Deciduous Shrub, Evergreen Shrubs, Evergreen Tree, Flowering Shrubs, Perennials & Annuals, Evergreen Tree, Tall Shrub, Evergreen Shrub, Perennials & Annuals, Flowering Shrub, Lawn, Evergreen Tree, Evergreen Shrubs, Evergreen Shrubs, Flowering Shrubs, Flowering Shrub, Evergreen Shrub Mass, Deciduous Shrub, Perennials & Annuals, Ground Cover, Perennials & Annuals, Evergreen Shrubs, Patio, Walk, Pergola, Evergreen Shrubs, Perennials & Annuals, Vines, HOUSE, Perennials, Evergreen Trees, Light, Flowering Evergreens, GARAGE, Perennials & Annuals, ENTRY, Walk, Walk, Perennials, Trees, Evergreen Shrubs, Perennials, Evergreen, Perennials, DRIVEWAY, Evergreen Shrubs

SPECIALTY STRUCTURES

Vivacious Vines—Visitors may have a difficult time deciding which way to enter house. Although most of us are socialized to go the front door, the vine-covered pergola looks so inviting that your visitor may decide to try the patio first.

Structures for supporting vines can introduce a tremendous amount of interest to your property. They can offer any color of the rainbow, variegated or lush green leaves of every size and shape, and fruits from edible to incredible. Their growth habits can range from invasive to timid. Some vines will make their own way by clinging and climbing, while others need a little help and training.

Use vines as a wall, fence, or ground cover and grow them as an annual, perennial, deciduous or evergreen woody plant.

SPECIALTY STRUCTURES

Tri-Level Deck—The nicest thing about decking is not that it enhances the look of any home, or that it creates outdoor living space, or even that it is adaptable to any terrain. It's that decking can be used on all planes.

One of the guidelines for garden design is to consider plants and structures for ground, vertical and overhead planes. Probably the easiest building material with which to achieve this goal is wood.

Tri-level deck, trellis and trees fill this design from ground to sky. The results are a three-story garden with floor, walls and cathedral ceiling.

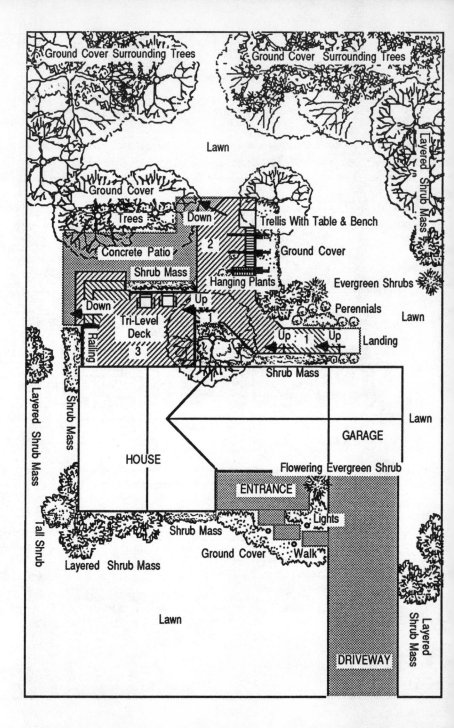

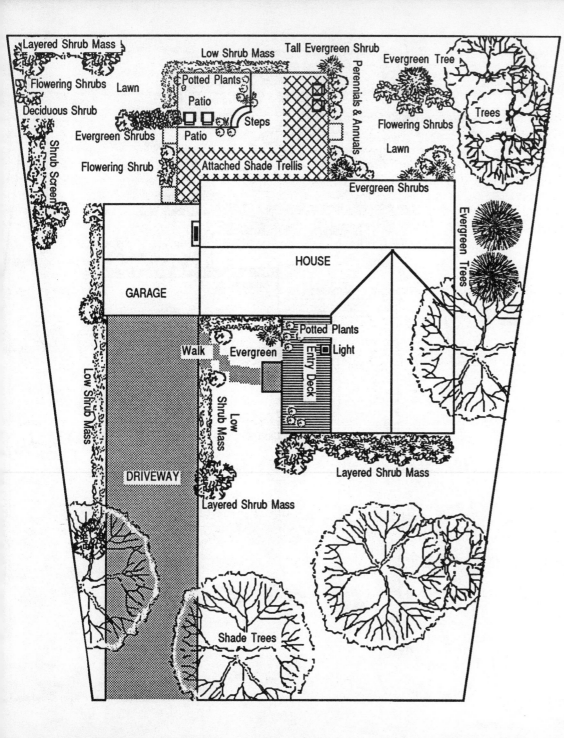

Layered Shrub Mass
Flowering Shrubs Lawn
Deciduous Shrub
Evergreen Shrubs
Flowering Shrub
Shrub Screen
Low Shrub Mass
Potted Plants
Patio
Patio
Steps
Attached Shade Trellis
Low Shrub Mass Tall Evergreen Shrub
Perennials & Annuals
Evergreen Tree
Flowering Shrubs
Lawn
Trees
Evergreen Shrubs
Evergreen Trees
GARAGE
HOUSE
Walk Evergreen
Low Shrub Mass
Potted Plants
Entry Deck Light
DRIVEWAY
Layered Shrub Mass
Layered Shrub Mass
Shade Trees

SPECIALTY STRUCTURES

Sun/Shade—A little innovative thinking can go a long way. The patio has two levels and a lattice-work shade trellis. Level changes offer the opportunity to use stepped plant arrangements and to create two separate patio areas. The shade trellis offers further separation. Using one basic structure, two vastly different living areas are formed.

Raised sun deck and shaded sitting area attached to house offer smooth circulation between house and patio and furnish easy access for entertaining or dining. Plants in containers can be easily taken indoors during inclement weather. Container plants can also be moved around and rearranged from time to time.

SPECIALTY STRUCTURES

Contemporary Flow—This design has simple, clean lines and is balanced with three grouping of trees. Use small flowering trees for a real show when in bloom.

The front entrance of the house is set off with two islands of plantings to enhance house from the street.

Main use area of back yard has been divided into two sections, one complementing the other. A contemporary outer patio curves into a more classical structure. Grill, counter and benches make a comfortable setting for almost any occasion.

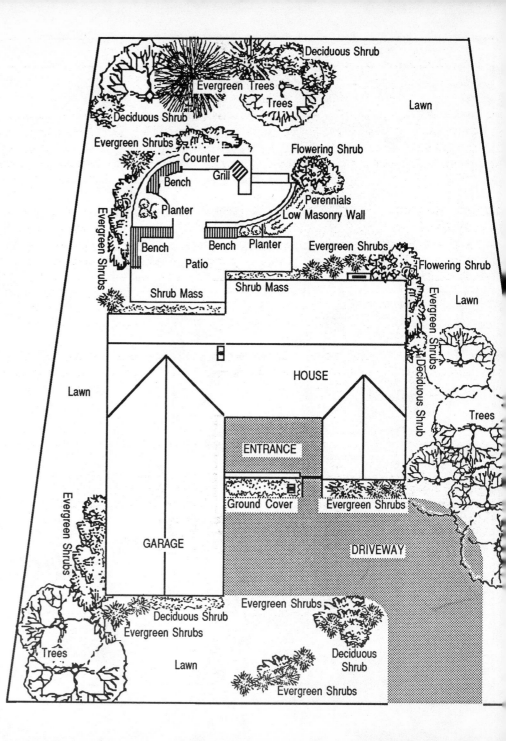

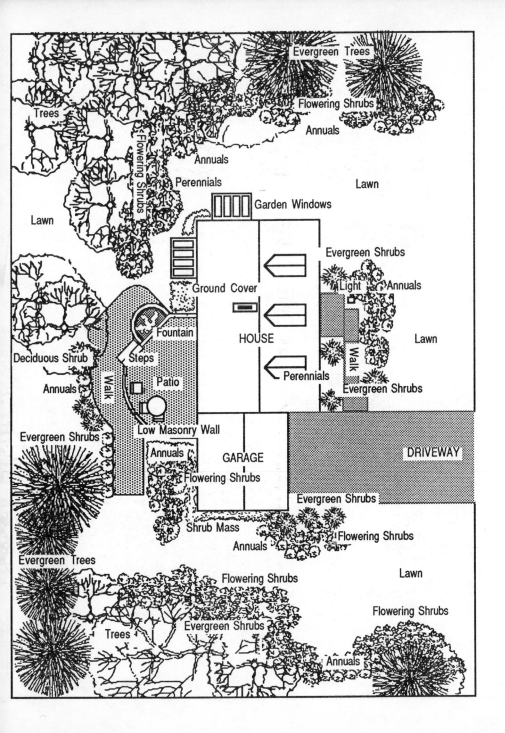

Evergreen Trees

Flowering Shrubs

Annuals

Trees

Annuals

Perennials

Lawn

Flowering Shrubs

Lawn

Garden Windows

Evergreen Shrubs

Ground Cover

Light

Annuals

Fountain

HOUSE

Lawn

Deciduous Shrub

Steps

Walk

Perennials

Annuals

Walk

Patio

Evergreen Shrubs

Low Masonry Wall

Evergreen Shrubs

Annuals

GARAGE

DRIVEWAY

Flowering Shrubs

Evergreen Shrubs

Shrub Mass

Flowering Shrubs

Annuals

Evergreen Trees

Lawn

Flowering Shrubs

Flowering Shrubs

Trees

Evergreen Shrubs

Annuals

SPECIALTY STRUCTURES

Bon Vivant—Well-traveled admirers of gardens will want a design of this sort for their own homes.

Color lights up the yard, just as color lights up a painter's canvas, and water has one of the highest priority levels of all garden features.

The tiered patio, fountain and flower beds aren't the only features either. Trees bring the garden into people proportion and create comfort in the garden. Garden windows allow excellent light indoors as well, allowing you to grow plants of your choice.

SPECIALTY STRUCTURES

Trellised Entry—The trellised entry and trellised deck are simple structures, but extremely warm and inviting features. The open simplicity of this design is indicative of the oriental style.

Three gardens with large stones and dwarf conifers provide an eastern flavor to terraced and rear decks. Three is a very popular number for oriental garden design.

To complete the authenticity of this design, use the grill as a hibachi, remove your shoes, sit on deck floor, and eat with chopsticks.

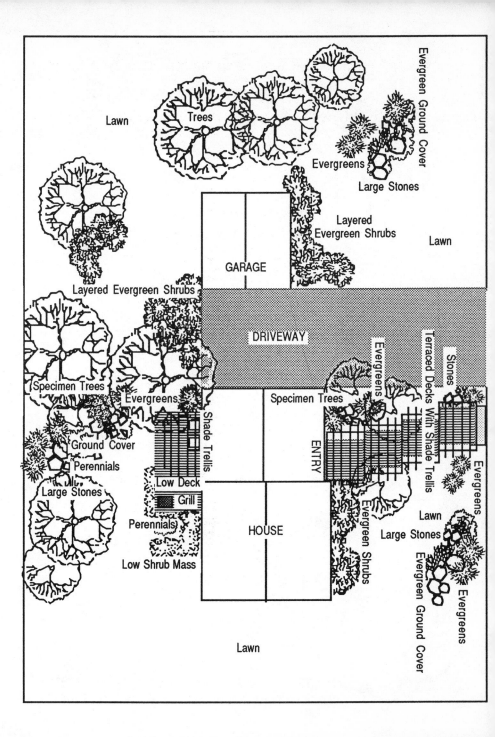

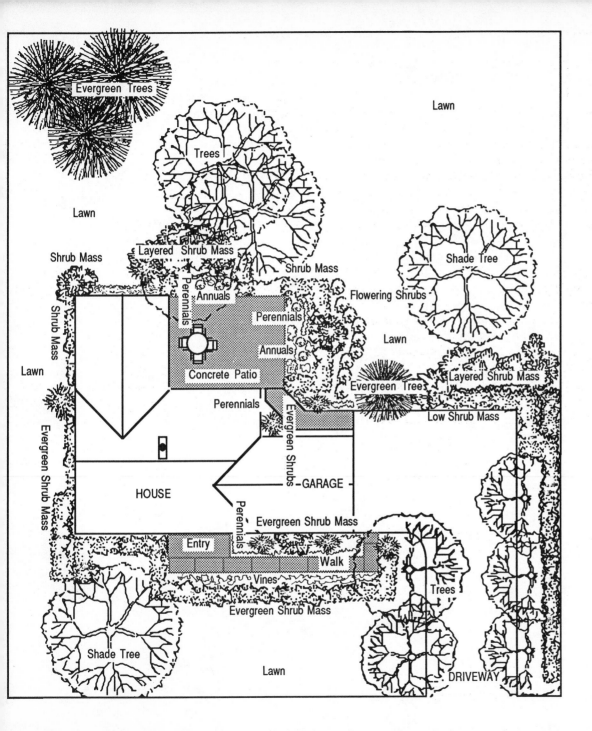

Evergreen Trees

Lawn

Trees

Lawn

Shade Tree

Shrub Mass

Layered Shrub Mass

Shrub Mass

Perennials

Annuals

Flowering Shrubs

Shrub Mass

Perennials

Lawn

Annuals

Layered Shrub Mass

Lawn

Concrete Patio

Evergreen Trees

Perennials

Low Shrub Mass

Evergreen Shrubs

Evergreen Shrub Mass

HOUSE

GARAGE

Perennials

Evergreen Shrub Mass

Entry

Walk

Vines

Trees

Evergreen Shrub Mass

Shade Tree

Lawn

DRIVEWAY

SCREENING

A Professional Job—House is screened on driveway side. Shrub mass softens hedge around back corner of drive. In the rear, the screening is moved in closer to the patio to create a smaller, more intimate space.

The finest public gardens design ornate enclosed spaces like this one, and you can reproduce the concept yourself. If you are just beginning, get around and see what others have done. Go to arboreta and gardens and take notes. Use plants that appeal to you.

Experiment with the plants you decide to use. Try different ones and different arrangements. Within several years you'll be a pro and have an ornate garden of your own.

SCREENING

Historically Sound—Tree and shrub masses can effectively screen a garden from almost anything. With clever pool house and container plant placement, privacy can become even more pronounced. The pool is situated to maximize screening from house as well.

The atrium or inner courtyard implies strong inward orientation, giving the enclosure an introspective nature. This is representative of Greek and Roman Peristyle design.

Both pools and atriums are time-tested structures that have been used in landscape design for over 2,000 years.

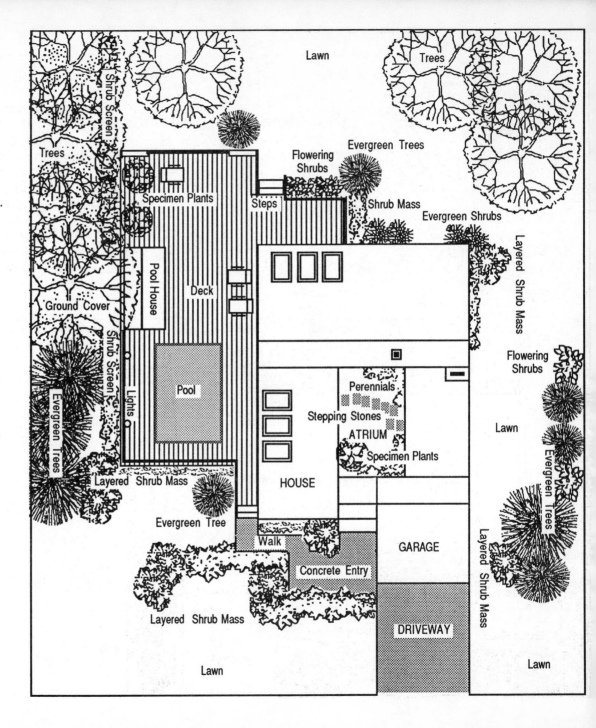

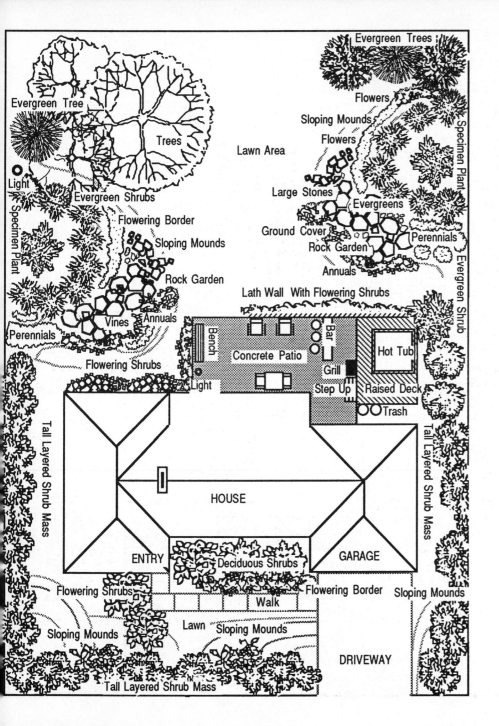

SCREENING

Islands of Interest—Hot tub situated close to the property line would make most people want a well-screened area. Why not build one with planting mounds?

Topsoil and large stones are used to elevate islands of interest for screening. The rise and fall of the land imitates natural contours and rock outcroppings.

The beds are so ornamental that screening becomes of secondary value for this design. The mounded beds are mainly aesthetically pleasing points of interest.

SCREENING

Magical Forest—In this plan, you feel like you live on the edge of an evergreen forest. Closely placed trees and shrubs will form a dense planting, and anyone's guess of what lies beyond would be as good as yours.

This is where the principle of mystery comes into play in the garden. Let your imagination run away. Fantasize a magical place, an alpine resort, a wooded retreat, or even the forest of Hansel and Gretel's gingerbread house. These can all be fun fantasies for young children, but being based in adult reality, you know that you just walk around and investigate further if necessary.

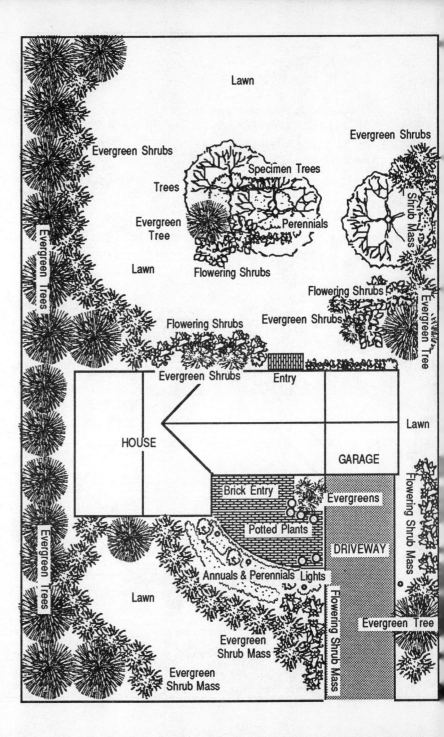

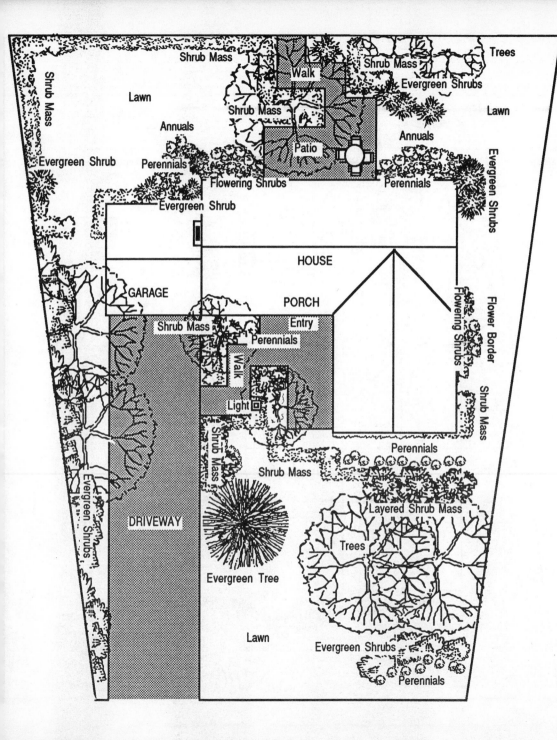

Trees

Shrub Mass

Shrub Mass

Walk

Evergreen Shrubs

Lawn

Lawn

Shrub Mass

Shrub Mass

Annuals

Annuals

Evergreen Shrub

Perennials

Patio

Flowering Shrubs

Perennials

Evergreen Shrub

Evergreen Shrubs

HOUSE

GARAGE

PORCH

Flowering Shrubs

Flower Border

Shrub Mass

Entry

Shrub Mass

Perennials

Walk

Light

Shrub Mass

Perennials

Shrub Mass

Layered Shrub Mass

Evergreen Shrubs

DRIVEWAY

Trees

Evergreen Tree

Lawn

Evergreen Shrubs

Perennials

SCREENING

Strategic Design—Create a good screen if you don't want to look out onto a busy street. A walk that winds to the front door will form openings where plants can be placed. This will partially hide a direct line of sight from the house, create a useful screen, and help define the entry.

Other trees and bedding areas are strategically designed to enhance house and entries as well. The line of sight along the left side of property has been totally blocked—a highly effective treatment for screening close neighbors, a commercial property or an unsightly lot.

SCREENING

Room Addition—Walled lawn and patios create a private garden close to the house. Because the area is so well enclosed, it can be used for everyday living. When the weather permits, dine, visit, watch T.V., or just relax in the privacy of an outdoor room.

The patio is built of concrete patio block. The wide variety of paving materials available today warrants looking around to pick favorites before patio installation.

Trees and massed shrubbery soften the wall line from inside and out to achieve tight enclosure without harsh steepness.

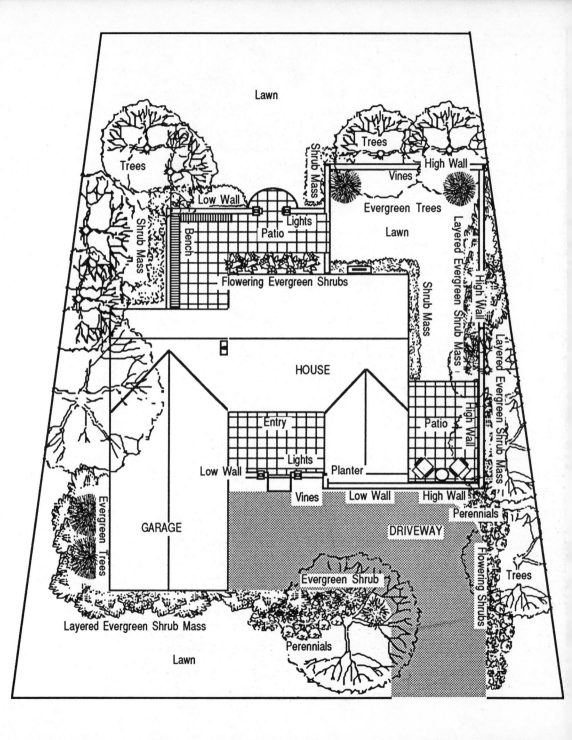

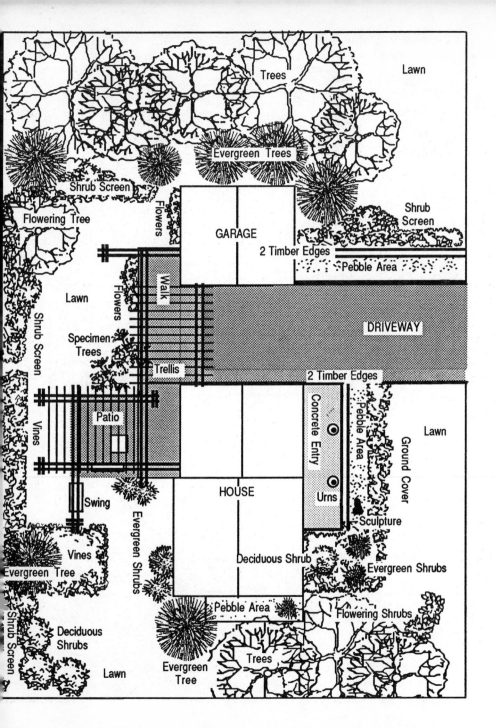

Lawn

Trees

Evergreen Trees

Shrub Screen

Flowering Tree

Flowers

GARAGE

Shrub Screen

2 Timber Edges

Pebble Area

Lawn

Flowers

Walk

Shrub Screen

Specimen Trees

Trellis

DRIVEWAY

2 Timber Edges

Pebble Area

Patio

Vines

Concrete Entry

Ground Cover

Lawn

Shrub Screen

Swing

HOUSE

Urns

Vines

Evergreen Shrubs

Sculpture

Evergreen Tree

Deciduous Shrub

Evergreen Shrubs

Shrub Screen

Deciduous Shrubs

Pebble Area

Flowering Shrubs

Lawn

Evergreen Tree

Trees

SCREENING

Open Enclosure—The overhead trellis creates open enclosure and ties the house to the garage. This theme is carried to the rear yard with trellised patio, swing and vines. Vines have a dense growth habit, and their low mounded nature offers implied enclosure.

Trees on side of house screen the property, but the lower limbs should be pruned above eye level for safety, aesthetics and to see the landscaping beyond.

Even front entry has an open feel because of the stone beds and urn arrangement. The trellis theme is carried to the front yard as well. Double timber edging is used to match material in shade trellis.

SCREENING

Frankly Formal—Take a tour of your yard. You've got it; you might as well use it. Table and chairs afford you the opportunity. A formal walk is intraplanted with small deciduous trees, lined with flowers and bordered by a narrow evergreen screen.

The formality of this design depends upon meticulously maintained and manicured plantings. A formal design is a pleasure to behold when it's been cared for properly, but that means weeding, pruning, pinching, fertilizing, mowing, mulching, edging, and more. It's a lot of work, but it's worth it.

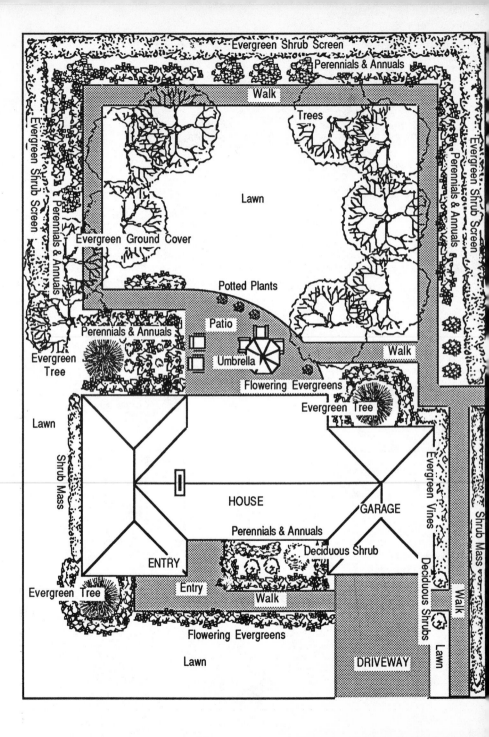

Part III
PLANT LISTS

PART III

The following lists represent a cross section of plants that grow throughout North America. They are arranged in categories that match the labels on the 101 designs in Part II. The list is alphabetized by common name for the benefit of the homeowner or non-horticulturist who may more easily recognize the plant. Common names are easier to read, and many times they will offer some hint about a special charactersitic the plant may have, such as Red Bud, Snow Bell, Spicebush, Sweetshrub, Lily Turf, and so on.

The difficulty in using common names is that they are sometimes used to denote several different species of plants. Therefore, the botanical name is given next to the common name to ensure clarity.

Several other factors are helpful to know when choosing a plant. They are hardiness zone, light requirement, and special use or characteristic, which are listed here in the preceding order following the botanical name. Light requirement is shown by SU (Sun), PS (Partial Sun), SH (Shade).

Hardiness zone is determined by the lowest temperature the plants will survive. The number directly next to the botanical name of each plant corresponds to a number on the Arnold Arboretum Hardiness Zone Map shown on page 120. Note also that lowest temperatures for each zone are given on the map.

Use this plant list to select plants and further stimulate your own ideas.

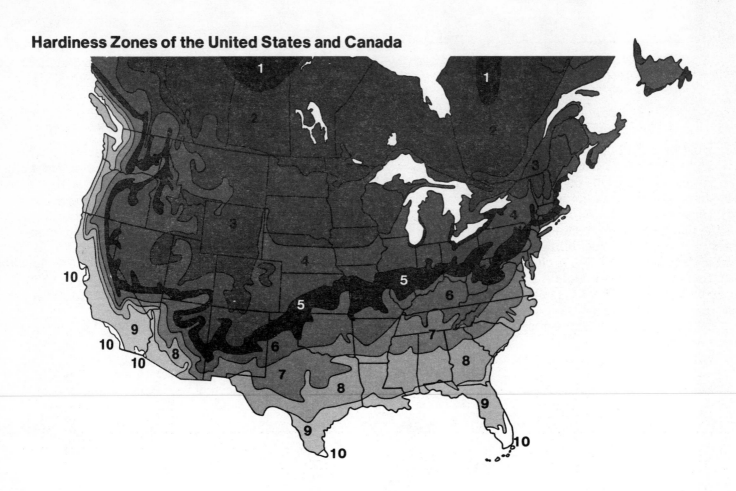

Hardiness Zones of the United States and Canada

Arnold Arboretum Hardiness Zone	Range of Average Annual Minimum Temperature (°F)	USDA Hardiness Zone
1	Below −50F	1
2	−50F to −45F	2a
	−45F to −40F	2b
	−40F to −35F	3a
3	−35F to −30F	3b
	−30F to −25F	4a
	−25F to −20F	4b
4	−20F to −15F	5a
	−15F to −10F	5b
5	−10F to −5F	6a
6	−5F to 0F	6b
	0F to 5F	7a
7	5F to 10F	7b
8	10F to 15F	8a
	15F to 20F	8b
9	20F to 25F	9a
	25F to 30F	9b
10	30F to 35F	10a
	35F to 40F	10b

Use this map only as a general guide. Consult your local nurseryman, garden club, county extension agent or state cooperative extension service for more exact information in your area regarding average annual minimum temperatures and frost dates. Climate zones illustrated here may vary slightly because precise weather patterns can change from year to year, and your own individual microclimate may not match this map.

SHADE TREES (40'–100')

Common Name	Botanical Name	Hardiness Zone	Light	Characteristic and/or Use
Alder, European or Common	Alnus glutinosa	3–7	PS	Wet areas
Alder, White	Alnus incana	2–7	PS	Wet areas
Ash, Black	Fraxinus nigra	2	SU	Wet areas
Ash, Flowering	Fraxinus ornus	5–6	SU	Fragrant flowers
Ash, Green	Fraxinus pensylvanica	3–9	SU	For tough to grow areas
Ash, Narrow Leaf	Fraxinus augustifolia	5	SU	Specimen
Beech, American	Fagus grandifolia	3–9	SU	Specimen, large areas
Beech, European	Fagus sylvatica	4–7	SU	Specimen, prune as hedge
Buckeye, Yellow	Aesculus octandra	3–8	SU	Fall color, flower
Butternut	Juglans cinerea	3–7	SU	Nut tree
Castor Aralia	Kalopanax pictus	4–7	SU	Large-leaved shade tree
Chestnut, Chinese	Castanea mollissima	4–8	SU	American chestnut replacement
Coffeetree, Kentucky	Gynocladus dioicus	3–8	SU	Interesting large space tree
Corktree, Amur	Phellodendron amurense	3–7	SU	Open crown, interesting bark
Elm, Chinese	Ulmus parvifolia	4–9	SU	American elm replacement
Filbert, Turkish	Corylus colurna	4–7	SU	Nice habit, edible nut
Ginko	Ginko biloba	3–8	SU	Good city tree & fall color
Gum, Black	Nyssa sylvatica	3–9	SU	Specimen, fall color
Hackberry, Common	Celtis occidentalis	3–8	SU	Good in wind & dry soils, Midwest
Hardy Rubber Tree	Eucommia ulmoides	4–7	SU	Pest free, Midwest locale
Hazel	Corylus colurna	4–7	SU	Few pests, lawn, city
Honeylocust, Common Thornless	Glenditsia triaconthos var. inermis	3–9	SU	Casts light shade
Hornbeam, European	Carpinus betulus	4–7	PS	Fall color
Horsechestnut, Common	Aesculus hippocastanum	3–7	SU	Flowers, large spaces
Katsuratree	Cercidiphyllum japonicum	4–8	SU	Fall color, large specimen
Linden, Littleleaf	Tilia cordata	3–7	SU	Can prune into hedge
Linden, Silver	Tilia tomentosa	4–7	SU	Heat & drought resistant
Locust, Black	Robinia pseudoacacia	3–8	SU	Grows anywhere
Magnolia, Cucumbertree	Magnolia acuminata	3–8	SU	Large leaves, large areas
Maple, Red	Acer rubrum	3–9	SU	Excellent fall color
Maple, Sugar	Acer sacchrum	3–8	SU	Excellent fall color, not cities
Oak, Burr	Quercus macrocarpa	2–8	SU	Specimen for very large areas
Oak, Chestnut	Quercus prinus	4	SU	Drought resistant, poor soils
Oak, English	Quercus robur	4–8	SU	For large areas
Oak, Laurel	Quercus laurifolia	6–9	SU	Specimen shade tree, smaller properties
Oak, Live	Quercus virginiana	7–10	SU	Specimen shade tree, larger properties
Oak, Pin	Quercus paltutris	4–8	SU	Nice pyramidal habit, residential landscape
Oak, Red	Quercus rubra	4–8	SU	Fast-growing shade tree
Oak, Sawtooth	Quercus acutissima	6–9	SU	Medium size, female flowers
Oak, Shingle	Quercus imbricaria	4–8	SU	Good in Midwest, can be used as hedge
Oak, Water	Quercus nigra	6–9	SU	Wet areas
Oak, Willow	Quercus pnellas	5–9	SU	Clean, good lawn tree

Common Name	Botanical Name	Hardiness Zone	Light	Characteristic and/or Use
Pagodatree, Japanese	Sophora japonica	4–8	SU	Flowers late summer, city tree
Pistache, Chinese	Pistacia chinensis	6–9	SU	Nice fall color and habit
Poplar, Japanese	Populus maxinowiczii	3–9	SU	Broad-spreading leaf, Midwest
Rubber Tree, Hardy	Eucommia ulmoides	4–7	SU	Deep green leaf, Midwest
Sweetgum, American	Liquidamber styraciflua	5–9	SU	Fall color, lawn tree, large areas
Wingnut, Caucasian	Pterocarya fraxinifolia	5–8	SU	Medium specimen shade tree
Yellowwood, American	Cladrastis lutea	3–8	SU	Showy flowering shade tree
Zelkova, Japanese	Zelkova serrata	5–8	SU	Elm substitute, fall color

SMALL/FLOWERING/SPECIMEN TREES (UNDER 40')

Common Name	Botanical Name	Hardiness Zone	Light	Characteristic and/or Use
Apricot, Manchurian	Prunus mandshurica	3	SU	Early flowers
Aralia, Japanese	Aralia elata	3–9	PS	Unique specimen
Birch, Asian White	Betula platyphylla	5	SU	May be borer resistant, specimen
Birch, Chinese Paper	Betula albo-sinensis	5	SU	Orange bark, specimen
Birch, Dwarf	Betula nana	2	SU	2-4' tall, rock gardens
Birch, Paper	Betula papyrifera	2–6	SU	White bark, fall color
Birch, River	Betula nigra	4–9	SU	Large birch, borer resistant
Birdcherry, European	Prunus padus	3	SU	Fragrant flowers, early to leaf out
Cherry, Bell-flowered	Prunus campanulata	6–9	SU	Fall color, flower
Cherry, Higan	Prunus subhirtella	4–8	SU	Graceful, flower
Cherry, Japanese Flowering	Prunus serrulata	6	SU	Flower
Cherry, Purpleleaf Sand	Prunus x cistena	2–8	SU	Hardiest purple leaf
Cherry, Sargent	Prunus sargentii	4–7	SU	Flowers, fall color, large
Cherry, Yoshino	Prunus x yedoensis	5–8	SU	Made D.C. famous for cherry blossoms
Crabapple, Flowering (Many Species)	Malus (Many Species)	3–8	SU	Flowers, many growth habits
Devil's Walking Stick	Aralia spinosa	4–9	SU	Pollution tolerant, thorny
Dogwood, Cornelian Cherry	Cornus mas	4–8	PS	Early flower, mass together
Dogwood, Flowering	Cornus florida	6–9	PS	Specimen patio tree
Dogwood, Kousa	Cornus kousa	5–8	SU	Specimen, good near house
Dogwood, Walter	Cornus walteri	5	PS	Specimen, bark interest
Dove-tree	Davidia involucrata	6–8	SH	Specimen, flower
Enkianthus, Red Vain	Enkianthus campanulata	4–7	PS	Specimen, flower, fall color
Franklin Tree	Franklinia alatamaha	5–8	SU	Specimen, fall color, flower
Fringetree, White	Chionanthus virginicus	3–9	SU	Specimen or groupings
Goldenchain Tree	Laburnum x watereri	5–7	PS	Sun, but protected, flower
Goldenraintree, Panicled	Koelreuteria paniculata	5–9	SU	Patio tree, late flower

Common Name	Botanical Name	Hardiness Zone	Light	Characteristic and/or Use
Hawthorn, Cockspur	Crataegus crusgalli	3–7	SU	2″ thorns, fall color
Hawthorn, Washington	Crataegus phaenopyrun	3–8	SU	Fruit, fall color, specimen
Hophornbeam, American	Ostrya viginiana	3–9	PS	Graceful, city use
Hoptree	Ptelea trifoliata	3–9	PS	Small, low branching habit
Hornbeam, American	Carpinus caroliniana	2–9	SH	Wet soil, shade
Horsechestnut, Red	Aesculus x carnea	3–7	SU	Red showy flowers
Lilac, Japanese Tree	Syringa reticulata	3–7	SU	Specimen tree
Maakia, Amur	Maakia amurensis	3–7	SU	Flowers late summer
Magnolia, Saucer	Magnolia x soulangiana	4–9	SU	Early showy flower, specimen
Magnolia, Star	Magnolia stellata	3–8	SU	Earliest magnolia flower specimen
Magnolia, Sweetbay	Magnolia virginiana	5–9	PS	Fragrant flowers, wet areas
Maple, Amur	Acer ginnala	2–7	SU	Small specimen, container
Maple, Full Moon	Acer japonicum	5	SU	Fall color
Maple, Hedge	Acer campestre	4–8	SU	Specimen, fall color
Maple, Japanese	Acer palmatum	5–8	SU	Specimen, many forms
Maple, Paperbark	Acer griseum	4–8	SU	Fall color, peeling bark
Maple, Purpleblow	Acer truncatum	5–8	SU	Fall color, lawn
Maple, Tatarian	Acer tataricum	3–8	SU	Specimen
Maple, Trident	Acer buergeranum	5–8	PS	Fall color, specimen
Mountainash, European	Sorbus aucuparia	3–6	SU	Handsome fruit, many diseases
Mountainash, Korean	Sorbus alnifolia	3–7	SU	Excellent for flowers & fruit
Oak, Chinese Evergreen	Quercus myrsinifolia	7–9	SU	Small garden tree, evergreen
Olive, Russian	Elaeagnus augustifolia	2–7	SU	Gray foliage, salt tolerant
Parasol Tree, Chinese	Firmiana simplex	7–9	SU	Very large leaves
Parrotia, Persian	Parrotia persica	4–8	SU	Pest free, specimen
Pear, Bradford	Pyrus calleryana 'Bradford'	4–8	SU	Flower, dense, shiny leaf
Pear, Chinese Sand	Pyrus pyrifolia	5–8	SU	Large, good flowering display
Pear, Ussurian	Pyrus ussuriensis	3–8	SU	Large hardy specimen
Plum, Flowering	Prunus cerasifera	3–8	SU	Red leaves, fragrant flowers
Quince, Chinese	Pseudocydonia sinensis	5–6	SU	Fragrant fruit, peeling bark
Redbud, Chinese	Cercis chinensis	6–9	PS	Extremely showy flowers
Redbud, Eastern	Cercis canadensis	4–9	PS	Flowers early, good in natural setting
Sassafras, Common	Sassafras albidum	4–8	SU	Fragrant stem, good in natural setting
Serviceberry, Downy	Amelanchier arborea	4–9	SU	White flowers, fall color
Silverbell, Carolina	Halesia carolina	4–8	SU	Natural settings
Snowbell, Japanese	Styrax japonicus	5	SU	Flowers, specimen
Soapberry, Western	Sapindus drummondii	6–9	SU	Fall color, dry areas
Sourwood	Oxydendron arboreum	5–9	PS	Summer flowers, fall color
Stewartia, Japanese	Stewartia pseudocamellia	5–8	PS	Good flower, bark & fall color
Stewartia, Mountain	Stewartia ovata	5–9	PS	Good flower, bark & fall color
Sumac, Flameleaf	Rhus copallina	4–9	SU	Fall color, specimen
Sumac, Staghorn	Rhus typhina	3–8	SU	Fall color, mass over large area
Yellowwood, Japanese	Cladrastis platycarpa	5–8	SU	Showy flower, disease free

EVERGREEN TREES (15′ AND OVER)

Common Name	Botanical Name	Hardiness Zone	Light	Characteristic and/or Use
Arborvitae, Giant	Thuja plicata	5–7	SU	Specimen hedge
Baldcypress, Common	Taxodium distichum (Deciduous conifer)	4	SU	Specimen, deciduous
Cedar, Atlas	Cedrus atlantica	6–9	SU	Specimen
Cedar, Deodar	Cedrus deodora	7–8	SU	Specimen
Cedar, of Lebanon	Cedrus libani	5–7	SU	Specimen
Chinafir, Common	Cunninghamia lanceolata	7–9	PS	Specimen, mass
Cryptomeria, Japanese	Cryptomeria japonica	6–8	SU	Specimen
Douglasfir	Pseudotsuga menziesii	4–6	SU	Specimen, windbreak
Falsecypress, Hinoki	Chamaecyparis obtusa	4–8	SU	Specimen, hedge
Falsecypress, Japanese	Chamaecyparis pisifera	3–8	SU	Golden variegation available
Falsecypress, Lawson	Chamaecyparis lawsonia	5–7	SU	Drooping branching habit
Fir, Fraser	Abies fraseri	4–7	SU	Specimen, Christmas tree substitute
Fir, White	Abies concolor	3–7	SU	Specimen, blue spruce substitute
Golden–larch	Pseudolarix kaempferi (Deciduous conifer)	4–7	SU	Specimen, cones
Hemlock, Canadian	Tsuga candensis	3–7	PS	Graceful, excellent hedge tree
Hemlock, Carolina	Tsuga caroliniana	4–7	PS	Whorled needles, rigid habit
Holly, American	Ilex opaca	5–9	SU	Winter berries, specimen
Holly, English	Ilex aquafolium	6–9	SU	Berries, specimen
Larch, European	Larix decidua (Deciduous conifer)	2–6	SU	Fall color, screen
Larch, Japanese	Larix kaempferi	4–7	SU	Ornamental for large areas
Magnolia, Southern	Magnolia grandiflora	6–9	SU	Specimen, wall plant
Pine, Austrian	Pinus nigra	4–7	SU	Specimen, windy locations
Pine, Bristlecone	Pinus aristata	4–7	SU	Specimen, rock garden
Pine, Eastern White	Pinus strobus	4–7	SU	Can be sheared, fine texture
Pine, Himalayan	Pinus wallichiana	5–7	SU	Long graceful needles
Pine, Japanese Black	Pinus thumbergiana	5–7	SU	Salt tolerant, windy areas
Pine, Japanese Red	Pinus densiflora	3–7	SU	Specimen, orangish bark
Pine, Japanese White	Pinus parviflora	4–7	SU	Hardy specimen
Pine, Korean	Pinus koraiensis	3–7	SU	Specimen
Pine, Lacebark	Pinus bungeana	4–8	SU	Peeling bark, specimen
Pine, Limber	Pinus flexilis	4–7	SU	Handsome and hardy
Pine, Macedonian	Pinus peuce	4–7	SU	Specimen
Pine, Red	Pinus resinosa	2	SU	Gorgeous tree for habit and bark
Pine, Swiss Stone	Pinus cembra	4–7	SU	Handsome bluish foliage
Redwood, Dawn	Metasequoia glyptostroboides	4–8	SU	Formal tree for large areas
Spruce, Colorado	Picea pungens	2–7	SU	Stiff habit, specimen
Spruce, Norway	Picea abies	2–7	SU	Graceful habit, windbreak
Spruce, Oriental	Picea orientalis	4–7	SU	Deep green, specimen
Spruce, Serbian	Picea omorika	4–7	SU	Weepy sterns, specimen
Spruce, White	Picea glauca	2–6	SU	Hardy, specimen
Umbrella-pine, Japanese	Sciadopitys verticillata	4–8	SU	Fleshy needles, specimen

EVERGREEN SHRUB SCREENS (5'–15')

Common Name	Botanical Name	Hardiness Zone	Light	Characteristic and/or Use
Arbovitae, American	Thuja occidentalis	2–8	SU	Narrow hedge
Arbovitae, Oriental	Platycladus orientalis	6–9	SU	Narrow hedge
Cypress, Leyland	X Cupressocyparis leylandii	6–10	SU	Fast growing
Guava, Pineapple	Feijoa sellowiana	8	SU	Foliage & flowers
Holly, Chinese	Ilex cornuta	7–9	SU	Winter berries, hedge
Holly, Japanese	Ilex crenata	5–6	SU	Good hedge & texture
Incensecedar, California	Calocedrus decurrens	5–8	SU	Handsome, formal
Juniper, Chinese	Juniperus chinensis	3–9	SU	Many forms, available in blue, yellow, green
Juniper, Rocky Mountain	Juniperus scopulorum	3–7	SU	Very blue, good in Midwest
Photinia, Chinese	Photinia serrulata	7–9	PS	New growth red, takes shearing
Photinia, Fraser	Photinia x fraseri	7–10	PS	Smaller than Chinese Photinia
Photinia, Japanese	Photinia glabra	7–9	PS	Smaller than Fraser Photinia
Podocarpus Yew	Podocarpus macrophyllus	8–10	SU	Deep green foliage, blue berry
Silverberry	Elaeagnus commutata	2–5	SU	Silver leaves
Viburnum, Leatherleaf	Viburnum rhytidophyllum	5–8	PS	Large leaf, rhododendron companion
Yaupon	Ilex vomitoria	7–10	SU	Persistent berries, narrow spreading habit
Yew, Anglojap	Taxus x media	4–7	SU	Dense spreading habit-mass or screen

DECIDUOUS SHRUB SCREEN (5'–15')

Common Name	Botanical Name	Hardiness Zone	Light	Characteristic and/or Use
Aralia, Fiveleaf	Acanthopanax sieboldianus	4–8	PS	Pollution tolerant, low maintenance
Cotoneaster, Hedge	Cotoneaster lucidus	3–7	SU	Tall narrow habit
Currant, Alpine	Ribes alpinum	2–7	PS	Hedge
Elliottia	Elliottia racemosa	5–8	SU	Flowers
Euonymus, Japanese	Euonymus japonicus	7–9	SH	Fast grower
Hardy-orange	Poncirus trifoliata	6–9	SU	Yellow fruit, thorny barrier
Holly, Common Winterberry	Ilex verticillata	3–9	SU	Berries persist without leaves, mass
Jasmine, Common White	Jasminum officinale	7–10	SU	Fragrant, deep green
Lilac, Chinese	Syringa x chinensis	2–7	SU	Fragrant, many colors
Lilac, Cutleaf	Syringa laciniata	5–8	SU	Fragrant, lobed leaf
Maple, Hedge	Acer campestre	4–8	SU	Must prune into hedge
Oak, Blue Japanese	Quercus glauca	8–9	SU	Large, widespread, slow growing
Oak, Columnar English	Quercus robur 'Fastigiata'	4–8	SU	Excellent narrow tree can grow 40'–50' tall
Privet, Amur	Ligustrum amurense	3–7	SU	Withstands heavy pruning
Privet, Border	Ligustrum obtusifolium	3–7	SU	Use in mass or hedge
Sapphireberry	Symplocos paniculata	4–8	SU	Attracts birds, can prune as tree
Viburnum, Arrowwood	Viburnum denatatum	2–8	SU	Hardy hedges
Viburnum, European Cranberrybush	Viburnum opulus	3–8	SU	Beautiful flowering shrub
Viburnum, Japanese	Viburnum japonicum	9	SU	Dense, narrow screen
Viburnum, Nannyberry	Viburnum lentago	2–8	PS	Background plant, attracts birds
Viburnum, Siebold	Viburnum sieboldii	4–7	SU	Specimen groupings, very large buildings
Viburnum, Wayfaringtree	Viburnum lantana	2–8	PS	Good flower, background

DECIDUOUS AND FLOWERING SHRUBS (3'–10')

Common Name	Botanical Name	Hardiness Zone	Light	Characteristic and/or Use
Abelialeaf, Korean	Abeliaphyllum distichum	5–8	SU	Early white fragrant flowers
Bamboo, Heavenly	Nandina domestica	6–9	PS	Foliage, specimen
Barberry, Japanese	Berberis thunbergii	4–8	SU	Foliage color, barrier
Barberry, Korean	Berberis koreana	3–7	SU	Berries, flowers, barrier
Barberry, Mentor	Berberis mentorensis	5–8	SU	Hedge, barrier
Barberry, Wintergreen	Berberis julianae	5–8	SU	Hedge, barrier
Bayberry, Northern	Myrica, pensylvanica	2–6	SU	Salt tolerant, mass
Beautyberry, Japanese	Callicarpa japonica	5–8	SU	Attractive fruit, perennial in North
Beautybush	Kolkwitzia amabilis	4–8	SU	Pink flower, plant alone
Bluebeard	Caryopteris x clandonensis	7	SU	Flower, aromatic
Blueberry, Highbush	Vaccinium carymbosum	3–7	SU	Fruit, shrub border
Blueberry, Rabbiteye	Vaccinium ashei	8–9	SU	Fruit, southern climates
Broom, Scotch	Cystisus scoparius	5–8	SU	Green stems, tolerant of poor soil
Buckeye, Bottlebrush	Aesculus parviflora	4–8	PS	Specimen or mass
Butterfly-bush	Buddleia davidii	5–9	SU	Summer flowers, cut flowers
Cinquefoil, Bush	Potentilla fruticosa	2–7	SU	Low border, flowers all summer
Clethra, Summersweet	Clethera alnifolia	3–9	PS	Summer flowers, shrub border
Cleyera, Japanese	Cleyera japonica	7–9	SH	Spring & winter leaf color
Cotoneaster, Spreading	Cotoneaster divaricatus	4–7	SU	Good summer & fall foliage
Crapemyrtle, Common	Lagerstroemia indica	7–9	SU	Specimen for bark & late flowering
Cyrilla, Swamp	Cyrilla racemiflora	5–10	SU	Good fall color, flowers
Daphne, Fragrant	Daphne odora	7–9	SU	Fragrant long-lasting flowers
Deutzia, Slender	Deutzia gracilis	4–8	SU	Hedge, mass
Dogwood, Redosier	Cornus sericea	2–8	PS	Red twigs, winter interest
Euonymus, Winged	Euonymus alatus	3–8	SU	Fall color, specimen, mass
Fatsia, Japanese	Fatsia japonica	8–10	SH	Large tropical looking leaf
Firethorn	Pyracantha coccinea	6–9	SU	Outstanding berries, espalier plant
Floweringquince	Chaenomeles speciosa	4–8	SU	Gorgeous flower, good barrier
Forsythia, Border	Forsythia x intermedia	4–8	SU	Early flower
Fothergilla, Large	Fothergilla major	4–8	SU	Disease free, shrub mass
Honeysuckle, Tatarian	Lonicera tatarica	3	SU	Many colors available
Honeysuckle, Winter	Lonicera fragrantissima	4–8	SU	Early flower, fragrant
Jasmine, Winter	Jasminum nudiflorum	6–10	SU	Winter flower, good cascading plant
Kerria, Japanese	Kerria japonica	4–9	SU	Yellow flower, all season tough
Lilac, Meyer	Syringa meyeri	3–7	SU	Dwarf lilac, pink flowers
Lilac, Persian	Syringa x persica	3–7	SU	Small lilac, lilac color
Mockorange, Sweet	Philadelphus coronarius	4–8	SU	Fragrant flowers
Pampas, Grass	Cortaderia selloana	7–9	SU	Tall grass, showy plume
Pearlbush	Exocordia racemosa	4–8	SU	Flower, mass with other shrubs
Peashrub, Chinese	Caragana sinica	5–7	SU	Early flower, fragrant stems
Peashrub, Siberian	Caragana arborescens	2–7	SU	Adaptable to many extremes of climates & soils

Common Name	Botanical Name	Hardiness Zone	Light	Characteristic and/or Use
Rose (Many Species)	Rosa (Many Species)	4–8	SU	Formal beds or thickets of thorns
Rose–of–Sharon	Hibiscus syriacus	5–8	SU	Summer flower, large areas in mass
St. Johnswort, Golden	Hypericum frondosum	5–8	SU	Summer flowers, exfoliating bark
St. Johnswort, Olympic	Hypericum olympicum	5–8	SU	Large flowers, grayish foliage
St. Johnswort, Shrubby	Hypericum prolificum	3–8	SU	Low hedge, bed edging
Smoketree, Common	Cotinus coggygria	5–8	SU	Purplish leaves, prune as tree
Spicebush	Lindera benzoin	4–9	SU	Stem fragrant, flower, fall color
Spirea, Bumald	Spiraea x bumalda	3–8	SU	Pink flower, mixed border
Spirea, Japanese White	Spiraea albaflora	4–8	SU	White flower, edging shrub
Stephanandra, Cutleaf	Stephanandra incisa	3–7	SH	Fall color, low mass or hedge
Sweetshrub, Common	Calycanthus floridus	4–9	SH	Fragrant, open natural habit
Viburnum, Burkwood	Viburnum x burkwoodii	3–8	SU	Fragrant, city specimen
Viburnum, Doublefile	Viburnum plicatum var. tomentosum	5–8	SU	White flower, specimen
Viburnum, Koreanspice	Viburnum carlesii	4–7	SU	Most fragrant and beautiful flower
Viburnum, Linden	Viburnum dilatatum	5–7	SU	Attractive manageable hedge
Viburnum, Witherod	Viburnum cassinoides	5–9	SU	Fall color, showy fruit
Weigela, Old Fashioned	Weigela floribunda	5–8	SU	Deciduous border, flowers
Winterberry, Common	Ilex verticillata	6–10	SU	Deciduous holly, showy berries
Winterhazel, Fragrant	Corylopsis glabrescens	5–8	SU	Early flower, fragrant
Wintersweet, Fragrant	Chimonanthus praecox	7–9	SU	Fragrant flowers, early
Witchhazel, Chinese	Hamamelis mollis	5–8	SU	Fall color, long-lasting early flowers
Witchhazel, Vernal	Hamamelis vernalis	4–8	SU	Long–lasting early flowers & fall color

EVERGREEN AND FLOWERING SHRUBS (3'–10')

Common Name	Botanical Name	Hardiness Zone	Light	Characteristic and/or Use
Abelia, Glossy	Abelia x grandiflora	6	PS	Mass
Alexandrian–laurel	Danae racemosa	8–9	SH	Cut stems, indoors
Andromeda, Japanese	Pieris japonica	5–8	PS	Flowers, mass
Andromeda, Mountain	Pieris floribunda	4	PS	Fragrant, rock gardens
Anise-tree, Florida	Ilicium floridanum	8–9	SH	Fragrant foliage
Anise-tree, Japanese	Ilicium anisatum	7–9	PS	Fragrant lustrous green leaves
Aucuba, Japanese	Aucuba japonica	7–10	SH	Variegated leaf, dense shade
Azalea (Many Species)	Rhododendron (Many Species)	5+ South	PS	Spring flower colors
Bayberry, Southern	Myrica cerifera	8–9	SU	Fragrant foliage, salt tolerant
Boxwood, Korean	Buxus sempevirens	6–9	SU	Hedge, specimen
Boxwood, Littleleaf	Buxus microphylla	6–9	SU	Hedge, formal garden
Buckwheat-tree	Cliftonia monophylla	7–9	SU	Fragrant flowers, shrub border
Camellia, Japanese	Camelia japonica	7–9	PS	Flower, specimen
Camellia, Sasanqua	Camelia sasanqua	7–9	PS	Flower, specimen
Cherrylaurel, Carolina	Prunus caroliniana	7–10	PS	Hedge, screen
Cherrylaurel, Common	Prunus laurocerasus	6	PS	Hedge, mass
Fetterbush	Leucothoe fantansiana	4–6	PS	Low-bordering shrub
Holly, Foster's	Ilex x attenuata	6–9	SU	Heavy fruit, specimen
Holly, Longstalk	Ilex pedunculosa	5	SU	Attracts birds, specimen
Holly, Meserve	Ilex x meserveae	7	SU	Specimen, cultivars
Inkberry	Ilex glabra	4–9	SU	Disease free, hedge
Jasmine, Cape	Gardenia jasminoides	8–10	SU	Fragrant flower, specimen
Lavender, Common	Lavandula augustifolia	5–9	SU	Fragrant flower, border hedge
Leucothoe, Coast	Leucothoe axilaris	4–6	SH	Deep green, shrub border
Leucothoe, Drooping	Leucothoe fantansiana	4–6	SH	Colorful leaf Var., border shrub
Loquat	Eriobotrya japonica	8–10	SU	Drought resistant, espalier
Loropetalum	Loropetalum chinensis	7–9	SH	Fragrant flower, deep green foliage
Mountain-laurel	Kalmia latifolia	4–9	SH	Showy flower, good for woods
Nandina	Nandina domestica	6–9	PS	Maroon leaf color, bamboo looking
Oleander	Nerium oleander	8–10	SU	Showy flower, pollution tolerant
Oregongrapeholly	Mahonia aquafolium	5–8	PS	Yellow flower, blue berries
Osmanthus, Fortune's	Osmanthus fortunii	7–9	PS	Hedge or specimen
Osmanthus, Holly	Osmanthus heterophyllus	7–9	PS	Hedge or specimen
Pieris, Japanese	Pieris japonica	5–8	PS	Beautiful flower, specimen
Pieris, Mountain	Pieris floribunda	4–8	PS	Fragrant flowers, rock gardens
Pine, Mugo	Pinus mugo var. mugo	2–7	SU	Low pine shrub
Pittosporum, Japanese	Pittosporum tobira	8	PS	Good massing shrub
Plant, Cast-iron	Aspidistra elatior	7–9	SH	Shrub edging for beds
Pomengranate	Panica granatum	7–10	PS	Fruit & excellent flower
Privet, Japanese	Ligustrum japonicum	7–10	PS	Glossy foliage, can shear

Common Name	Botanical Name	Hardiness Zone	Light	Characteristic and/or Use
Raphiolepsis, Yeddo	Raphiolepsis umbellata	7–10	SU	Low massing shrub
Rhododendron (Many Species)	Rhododendron (Many Species)	4+ South	SH	Colorful, coarse, natural habit
Rosemary	Rosmarinus officinalis	6	SU	Herb, good over edge of wall
Sandmyrtle, Box	Leiophyllum buxifolium	5	SU	Low rock garden plant
Santolina	Santolina chamaecyparissus	6–9	SU	Low hedge or edging shrub
Skimmia, Japanese	Skimmia japonica	7–8	SH	Red fruit, low mass
Yew, English	Taxus baccata 'Repandans'	6–7	SU	Low mass, good cascading plant
Yew, Japanese	Taxus cuspidata	4–7	SU	Deep green foliage, massing
Yucca, Soapweed	Yucca glauca	4	SU	Ridig leaf, showy flowers

DECIDUOUS GROUND COVERS

Common Name	Botanical Name	Hardiness Zone	Light	Characteristic and/or Use
Barberry, Paleleaf	Berberis canbidula	5–8	SU	Low 2' mass
Bunchberry	Cornus canadensis	2	SH	Fall color, fruit for birds
Cinquefoil	Potentilla verna 'Nana'	2–7	SU	Summer flower, yellow
Cotoneaster, Cranberry	Cotoneaster apiculatus	4–7	SU	Fruit, cascade over wall
Cotoneaster, Creeping	Cotoneaster adpressus	4–7	SU	Fruit, rock gardens
Cotoneaster, Rockspray	Cotoneaster horizontalis	4	SU	Low massing
Forsythia, Arnold Dwarf	Forsythia 'Arnold Dwarf'	5	SU	3' tall, vigorous spreader
Holly-fern, Japanese	Cyrtomium falcatum	8	SH	Foliage, true fern
Ivy, Boston	Parthenocisus tricuspidata	4–8	SH	Fall color, spring color
Rose, Memorial	Rosa wichuraiana	5–8	SU	Long prostrate canes, large banks
Sumac, Fragrant	Rhus aromatica	3–9	SU	Fragrant fall color
Thyme, Mother-of-	Thymus serpyllum	4	SU	Fragrant ground cover, rock garden
Woadwaxen	Genista tinctoria 'Plena'	4–7	SU	Green stems in winter, yellow color
Yellowroot	Xanthorhiza simplicissima	3–9	SU	Dense, 2' high mass

EVERGREEN GROUND COVER

Common Name	Botanical Name	Hardiness Zone	Light	Characteristic and/or Use
Ardisia	Ardisia japonica	8–9	SH	Tall dense mat
Azalea (Creeping)	Rhododendron (Hybrids)	5–7	PS	Flowering value near wooded areas
Bearberry	Arctostapylos uva–ursi	2–5	PS	Salt tolerant, fall color
Candytuft	Iberis sempervirens	4–8	SU	Early flower
Cotoneaster, Bearberry	Cotoneaster dammeri	5–8	SU	Fast growing, glossy carpet
Cotoneaster, Weeping Willowleaf	Cotoneaster salicifolius	6–8	SU	Cascade over walls
Euonymus, Wintercreeper	Euonymus fortunei	4–8	PS	Wall covering, low hedge
Grapeholly, Dwarf	Mahonia repens	5–8	PS	Green in summer, red in winter
Heath, Spring	Erica carnea	4–6	SU	Winter/spring flower, mass
Heather, Scotch	Calluna vulgaris	4–6	SU	Summer flower, mass
Huckleberry, Box	Gaylussacia brachycera	5	SH	Under rhododendron & pine
Ivy, English	Hedera helix	4–9	SH	Lush green, heavy shade
Juniper, Creeping	Juniperus horizontalis	3–9	SU	Many forms, available in blues, greens & yellows
Juniper, Japgarden	Juniperus procumbens	4–9	SU	Dwarf plant, blue-green
Juniper, Shore	Juniperus conferta	6–8	SU	Seashore, poor soils
Lilyturf, Creeping	Liriope spicata	4	PS	Grows in all light and soil
Lilyturf, Big Blue	Liriope muscari	4	PS	Thick leaved, bluish
Pachisandra, Alleghany	Pachisandra procumbens	4–9	SH	Wide leaved, bluish color
Pachisandra, Japanese	Pachisandra terminalis	4–9	SH	Handsome under trees
Pachistima, Canby	Pachistima canbyi	3–8	SU	Border planting around shrubs
Partridgeberry	Mitchella repens	3–9	SH	Very low to ground
Periwinkle, Common	Vinca minor	3–8	SH	Blue flower, lush shade carpet
Periwinkle, Large	Vinca major	7–9	SH	Blue flower, large leaves
St. Johnswort, Aaronsbeard	Hypericum calycinum	5–8	SU	Semi-evergreen, summer flower
Sweet Box	Sarcococca hookerana humilis	5–8	PS	Fragrant flowers, dense ground cover
Wintergreen, Creeping	Gaultheria procumbens	3	PS	Fragrant leaves, winter color

VINES

Common Name	Botanical Name	Hardiness Zone	Light	Characteristic and/or Use
Akebia, Fiveleaf	Akebia quinata	6–8	PS	Good vine for structures
Ampelopsis, Porcelain	Ampelopsis brevipedunculata	4–8	SU	Ornamental fruit, train on trellis
Bittersweet, American	Celastrus scandens	3–8	SU	Cut branches, container or very large spaces
Boston Ivy	Parthenocissus tricuspidata	4–8	SH	Fall color, spring color
Clematis (Many Species)	Clematis (Many Species)	3–8	SU	Beautiful long season flower
Crossvine	Anisostichus capreolata	6–8	SU	Flowers, red/purple in cold
Fatshedera	x Fatshedera lizei	8	SH	Large-leaved climber
Fig, Climbing	Ficus pumila	8–10	SU	Mats onto structure
Fleeceflower	Polygonum aubertii	4–7	PS	Quick cover where others won't
Honeysuckle, Goldflame	Lonicera x heckerotti	5	SU	Everblooming
Hydrangea, Climbing	Hydrangea anomala sub. peteolaris	4–7	SH	Winter flowers, good climber
Jasmine, Confederate	Trachelospermum jasminoides	8	SU	Fragrant
Jessimine, Carolina Yellow	Gelsemium sempervirens	6–9	SU	Bright yellow flowers, cascading habit
Kiwi Fruit	Actinidia chinensis	7–9	SU	Large leaves, fast grower
Pipe, Dutchman's	Aristolochia durior	4–8	PS	Screen on trellis
Silverlace, Vine	Polygonum aubertii	4–8	SU	Fine flower, resistant to climatic extremes
Tara Vine	Actinidia arguta	4	PS	Quick cover vine
Trumpetcreeper, Common	Campsis radicans	4–9	SU	Quick cover, orange trumpet flowers
Virginia Creeper	Parthenocissus quinqefolia	3–9	SH	Quick cover, fall cover
Wisteria, Japanese	Wisteria floribunda	4–9	SU	Heavy wood, excellent fragrant flower

PERRENIALS

Common Name	Botanical Name	Hardiness Zone	Light	Characteristic and/or Use
Adonis, Spring	Adonis vernalis	3	SU	Fine-textured yellow foliage, rock gardens
Ageratum, Hardy	Eupatorium coelestinum	3	PS	Blue summer flower
Alyssum	Aurinia saxatilis	3	SU	Early spring thorny yellow flowers
Anchusa	Anchusa azurea	3	SU	Tall, blue, can continue to bloom
Anthemis	Anthemis tinctoria	3	SU	Tall, yellow, continuous bloom
Artemisia	Artemisia schmidtiana	3	SU	Interesting silver foliage & mounted habit
Aster	Aster frikarti	4	SU	Tall, continuous bloom
Astilbe	Astilbea orendsi	4	SH	Red summer flower
Baby's-Breath	Gypsophila paniculata	3	SU	Wide spreading, good cutting & drying
Balloon Flower	Platycodon grandiflora	3	SU	Summer bloom, showy flower buds
Baptisia	Baptisia australis	3	SU	Attracts winter birds, use in mass
Bee-Balm	Monarda didyma	4	PS	Summer flower, tall, variety of colors
Bellis	Bellis perennis	3	PS	Early flower, reseeds itself annually
Bleeding Heart	Dicentra spectabilis	4	PS	Heart-shaped flowers, beautiful in early spring
Brunnera	Brunnera macrophylla	4	PS	Blue, not extremely hardy, reseeds well
Buttercups	Ranunculus (Many Species)	4	SU	Wildflower, yellow, many species
Butterfly Weed	Asclepias tuberosa	4	SU	Tall, orange, late summer
Campanula	Campanula (Many Species)	3	SU	Many sizes, blue or white bell-shaped flower
Candytuft	Iberis sempervirens	3	SU	Low, white, good bed edging
Centaurea	Centaurea montana	4	SU	Tall, silver foliage, blue flower
Cerastium	Cerastium tomentosum	2	SU	White flower, masses well as ground cover
Chinese Lantern	Physalis alkekengi	3	SU	Red lantern shape, use separately in garden
Chrysanthemum	Chrysanthemum morifolium	3–5	SU	Every color and shape blossom
Columbine	Aquilegia (Many Hybrids)	3	PS	Variety of colors, fan shaped foliage
Coralbells	Heuchera sanquinea	3	SU	Small pink flowers, good foliage
Coreopsis	Coreopsis (Many Species)	4	SU	Yellow, long blooming period
Daylilies	Hemerocallis (Many Species)	2	PS	Many colors, good summer foliage
Delphinium	Delphinium (Many Species)	3	SU	Many colors, rich soil, extremely tall
Dianthus	Dianthus (Many Species)	3–7	SU	Rock gardens, cutting, can bloom continuously
Doronicum	Doronicum cordatum	4	PS	Early bloom, yellow daisy-like flower
Felicia	Felicia amelloides	5	SU	Blue daisy look, mild winters
Feverfew	Chrysanthemum parthenium	3	SU	Cut flowers, continuous bloom
Flax	Linium flavum	4	SU	Yellow flower all summer
Fleabane	Erigeron (Many Species)	3	PS	Many species for different times of bloom
Gaillardia	Gaillardia aristata	3	SU	Cut flowers, many colors
Geranium	Geranium (Many Species)	4	SU	Reds, early flower, rock garden
Gerbera	Gerbera jamesoni	8	SU	Many colors, showy large blooms
Geum	Geum chiloense	5	SU	Red, mixed perennial border
Globeflower	Trollius europaeus	3	PS	Yellow, large ball flowers, cut flowers
Globe Thistle	Echinops exaltatus	4	SU	Tall, blue, place to back of other flowers
Helenium	Helenium autumnale	3	SU	Good late summer bloom for cutting
Heliopsis	Heliopsis helianthoides	3	SU	Late summer, up to 5′ tall
Helleborus	Helleborus orientalis	4	SH	Many colors, late winter bloom
Hosta	Hosta (Many Species)	3	SH	Good foliage, edging plant
Hypericum	Hypericum patulum	5	SU	Yellow, tall, mixed flower border

Common Name	Botanical Name	Hardiness Zone	Light	Characteristic and/or Use
Iris	Iris (Many Species)	3	SU	All colors and combinations, showy
Jacob's Ladder	Polemonium caeruleum	4	SH	Blue, reseeds well, spring
Jupiter's Beard	Centranthus ruber	4	SU	White, red, tall summer flower
Lamb's Ear	Stachys lanata	4	SU	White woody foliage, ground cover
Lavender	Lavandula angustifolia	5	SU	Blue, fragrant, herb garden
Leadwort	Ceratostigma plumbaginoides	6	PS	Blue, reddish fall color, ground cover
Lily, Hardy	Lilium (Many Species)	3	SU	Many colors & heights, bloom at different times
Lobelia	Lobelia cardinalis	2	SH	Summer/fall color, red
Loosestrife	Lythrum salicaria	3	PS	Range of reds, moist areas, naturalize
Lungwort	Pulmonaria saccharata	3	SH	Good foliage, pink flower, will spread
Lupine	Lupinus	4–7	SU	Variety of colors, cuttings & mixed borders
Monkshood	Aconitum carmichaeli	3	SU	Tall, late summer
Painted Daisy	Chrysanthemum coccineum	4	SU	White, red, pink, showy flower
Penstemon	Penstemon barbatus	4	PS	Rose colored, trumpet-shaped flowers
Peony	Paeonia (Many Species)	3	SU	Shrub-like, many colors, showy flower
Phlox, Tall	Phlox paniculata	4	SU	Tall, pink flower, cuttings
Poker Plant	Kniphofia uvaria	5	SU	Needs protection, very showy flowers
Poppy	Papover orientale	2	SU	Beautiful pinks, reds, oranges, whites
Potentilla 'Miss Wilmott'	Potentilla nepalensis	4–5	SU	Red-pink flower, edging
Primrose	Primula (Many Species)	3–5	SU	Many colors, early spring
Rudebekia	Rudebekia (Many Species)	3	SU	Yellow flower—like a black-eyed susan
Salvia, Hardy	Salvia (Many Species)	4	SU	Blue spikes summer & fall
Scabiosa	Scabiosa (Many Species)	5	SU	White, blue, pink—looks like a pin cushion
Sedum	Sedum (Many Species)	3	SU	Many sizes & colors, rock garden
Shasta Daisy	Chrysanthemum maximum	4	SU	Tall mass, shrub-like into summer
Stokesia	Stokesia laevis	5	SU	Late summer bloom, blue or white
Thermopsis	Thermopsis caroliniana	3	SU	Tall, yellow, summer
Thrift, Sea	Armeria maritima	3	SU	Showy flower, bed edging
Veronica	Veronica (Many Species)	3	SU	Long period of bloom, clip faded flowers
Violet	Viola odorata	4	PS	Fragrant pink bloom, long stem
Virginia Bluebells	Mertensia virginica	3	SH	Blue flower, early spring
Yarrow, Fern-leaved	Achillea filipendulina	3	SU	Yellow, cutting, drying—fern-like foliage

Common Name	Botanical Name	Light	Characteristic and/or Use
African Daisy	Dimorphotheca (Many Hybrids)	SU	Large blooms, many colors, cuttings
Alyssum	Lobrilaria maritima	PS	Fragrant, ground cover, rock gardens
Amaranth	Amaranthus (Many Species)	SU	Brilliant foliage, annual hedge
Anchusa	Anchusa capensis	SU	Medium height, blue, mass
Aster	Callistephus chinensis	PS	Many colors, cut flowers, moist
Begonia	Begonia semperflorens	PS	Foliage & flower color, bushy mass
Begonia, Tuberous	Begonia x tuberhybrids	SH	Brilliant colors, can be perennial
Black-Eyed Susan Vine	Thumbergia alata	PS	Light petals, dark centers, vining
Browallia	Browallia speciosa	PS	Blues, whites, cascade, hanging baskets
Calendula	Calendula officinalis	PS	Yellows, whites, full marigold look
Candytuft	Iberis (Many Species)	PS	All sizes, ground cover, rock garden, flower border
Carnation	Dianthus caryophyllus	PS	Cut flowers, prune blooms for continuous flowering
Cockscomb	Celosia plumosa	PS	Colorful foliage & flower, feathery flower
Coleus	Coleus blumei	SH	Colorful foliage, pinch flowers to keep foliage color
Cornflower	Centaurea cyanus	PS	Blue, pink, white, cutting & drying
Cosmos	Cosmos bipinnatus	PS	Whites & reds, other species available
Dahlberg Daisy	Dyssodia tenuiloba	SU	Fragrant foliage, withstands hot weather
Dahlia	Dahlia (Many Hybrids)	PS	All colors, big flower, 1′–2′ tall
Dusty Miller	Chrysanthemum ptarmiciflorum	PS	Silver gray foliage, edging
Flossflower	Ageratum houstoniatum	PS	Blue, white, edgings, flower border
Flowering Tobacco	Nicotiana (Many Species)	PS	Red, pink, white, fragrant, flower border
Fuchsia	Fuchsia magellanica	SH	Pink, white, purple, hanging baskets
Gazanice	Gazania rigens	PS	Bicolored flowers, showy for hot dry areas
Geranium	Pelargoniun x hortorum	SU	Hanging baskets, border, edging, showy
Impatiens	Impatiens wallerana	SH	Hanging baskets, edging, shrub effect
Lobelia	Lobelia erinus	PS	Hanging baskets, edging many shades of blue
Marigold	Tagetes patula	SU	Yellows to reds, fine-textured foliage mass
Monkey Flower	Mimulus (Many Hybrids)	PS	Yellow & red bicolor, showy flowers
Moss Rose	Portulaca grandiflora	SU	Very colorful, dry weather carpet
Ornamental Pepper	Capsicum annuum	PS	Yellow, red, white, colorful, edible fruit
Pansy	Viola (Many Species)	PS	Many colors, use in mass
Periwinkle	Vinca rosea	SU	Good flower and foliage, shrub-like
Petunia	Petunia x (Many Hybrids)	PS	Many colors, baskets, container gardens
Phlox	Phlox drummondii	PS	Clip faded blooms to keep full, rock gardens
Pinks	Dianthus chinensis	SU	Flowers edged in pink, cut flowers
Salpiglossis	Salpiglossis sinuata	PS	Deep colors, velvet texture, background
Salvia	Salvia (Many Species)	PS	Spike of flowers, mass, container garden
Snapdragon	Antirrhinum majus	PS	Many bright colors, mixed border or background
Spiderplant	Cleome hasslerana	SU	White or pink "spidery" flowers, June to August
Statice	Limonium (Many Species)	SU	Cut flowers, dried tiny flowers
Strawflower	Helichrysum bracteatum	SU	Many colors & bicolors, cutting & drying
Verbena	Verbena hortensis	PS	Many colors & hybrids, creeping & upright varieties
Wishbone Flower	Torenia fournieri	SH	Bicolored flower, pansy looking
Zinnia	Zinnia elegans	SU	Many colors and combinations, mass or flower border